ANTHROPOLOGICAL PAPERS



MUSEUM OF ANTHROPOLOGY, UNIVERSITY OF MICHIGAN
NO. 50

# FACTION AND CONVERSION IN A PLURAL SOCIETY: RELIGIOUS ALIGNMENTS IN THE HINDU KUSH

BY
ROBERT LEROY CANFIELD

ANN ARBOR
THE UNIVERSITY OF MICHIGAN, 1973

# PREFACE

THIS is a partial report of field work done between October 1966 and June 1968. That time was the climactic period of almost ten years of experience in Afghanistan. During the previous years there, when working as an educationalist, I acquired some skill in Afghan Persian which served me well when I returned to do ethnological research. I do not learn languages easily, and therefore was particularly fortunate to have spent much more time on language study than most anthropologists can give to it. My proficiency, therefore, was fairly good at the beginning of field work, and it of course improved with further practice; toward the end of my field work I was able to understand almost everything said between third parties.

The research was carried on without an interpreter, but I had some difficulty understanding the Hazara dialects of Persian, Hazaragi. This difficulty was most pronounced in my few interviews with older women. The dialect of the younger women posed less difficulty, and that of most men hardly any. As I learned much of the language from Hazaras, my Persian probably bears traces of Hazaragi that I do not distinguish from standard Afghan Persian.

My research strategy was dictated by the opportunities that fell to me. My family lived in Kabul, and I carried on field work by making treks into different areas of Bamian. During times when I was in Kabul I interviewed a number of persons from Bamian, and many of these interviews turned out to be especially valuable.

When in the field, I carried little more than a sleeping bag and several cans of fly spray, which were prized by my hosts. I was therefore closely dependent on local resources. I was invited to stay with local officials in the different substations of government and at first I did so. Gradually, however, I became more dependent on local hospitality and eventually hardly saw the officials. Most of my local hosts were friends or relatives of friends I had known in Kabul. As they were distributed in a number of neighborhoods, their hospitality enabled me to see most of the valleys of eastern Bamian, and of course most of all, to learn a great deal about their way of life. After a few months one person offered a room in his house as a permanent place to stay and I used it as a *pied-a-terre.*

For my second year in Bamian, I shifted the focus of my research to the market in the center of the Bamian basin. There I stayed in tea shops, and spent many long evenings discussing local affairs and problems. From the market I made journeys on foot into the southern highlands and other portions of the Tagaw plain. I also visited regions to the north and west.

I often travelled to Bamian by bus or truck because on the way I could meet people from diverse localities and backgrounds. Amid the dust and noise, the crush, the arguments and the long delays, there were superb opportunities to observe and befriend people which no other means of transport could provide.

During the course of the research and the writing of this report I have incurred many obligations. A training grant from the Foreign Area Fellowship Program supported the two years of field work, and with a supplementary grant from the Center for Near East and North African Studies supported a year of data sorting and writing. Many persons in Afghanistan assisted the research. A number of Bamian residents gave much time to explaining their economic circumstances and customs. Some explained in detail the kinds of problems they had. About a dozen persons repeatedly gave me their time in long, intensive interviews. Three persons—two Hazaras and a Tajik—travelled with me at different times and helped me understand what I saw and heard. The government officials were also cooperative. The research, of course, could not have been possible without the gracious permission of the Ministry of Foreign Affairs and the Ministry of Interior. To all the persons and agencies who made the research possible I am sincerely grateful.

The contribution of three scholars to the study of Hazaras deserves special acknowledgment in view of the few citations to their work in the text: Elizabeth Bacon, Klaus Ferdinand, and H. F. Schurmann. Dr. Bacon was the first anthropologist to do serious ethnographic work in central Afghanistan. Her field study of the Hazaras was hampered by awkward field circumstances and interrupted by the advent of World War II, but the material she gathered and the research she has done on Hazara affinities with other Mongol groups are basic resources on Hazara culture (see her 1951*a*, 1951*b*, 1958, and Hudson and Bacon, 1941). Aware of limitations in her Hazara material, she only used it schematically to support a broad argument, but generally her data are substantiated by mine.[1] Ferdinand has made two valuable studies of society in central Afghanistan, an ethnographic sketch of Hazara culture (1959), and an account of contemporary relations between the Hazaras and the Afghan nomads (1962). Schurmann

[1] The arguments developed by Dr. Bacon from her Hazara data also anticipated some subsequent theoretical developments. In her most ambitious work (1958) she distinguished segmentary lineage structure (which she called "tribal geneological organization" or *obok*) from clan structures, and suggested how it may be related to other forms of kinship organization. Also she stressed the importance of distinguishing the names of groups from their actual composition (cf. Sahlins 1965*a*).

(1962) studied an isolated group of Mongols in western Afghanistan who apparently have close affinities with the Hazaras. His attempt to relate the culture of these Mongols to other ethnic groups, though it suffers from an inadequate conception of the nature of ethnicity and culture change, is meritorious for its extensive coverage of much relevant literature.

I owe a special debt to my instructors at The University of Michigan for teaching me most of the anthropology I know and for patiently guiding my work on this study. The debt is perhaps greatest to Professor William Schorger who has counselled me through my entire doctoral program. By commenting in detail on two drafts of this manuscript, he has taught me much about how to explain myself. Professor Eric Wolf also read both drafts and made several necessary theoretical suggestions. Professor Aram Yengoyan saved me from some serious omissions. My debt to Professors Wolf and Marshall Sahlins is only partially evident in the references to their work.

To Irma Morose I owe thanks for typing this and most of another version of the thesis, and to Penny Ryan for preparing some of the maps. My debt to my wife surpasses words. She has supported and encouraged me during seven years of work on the doctor's degree. The least of her contributions to this thesis has been the typing of one full draft and portions of another. To her, and to my parents, I dedicate this work.

# TABLE OF CONTENTS

## LIST OF FIGURES

Page



## LIST OF TABLES

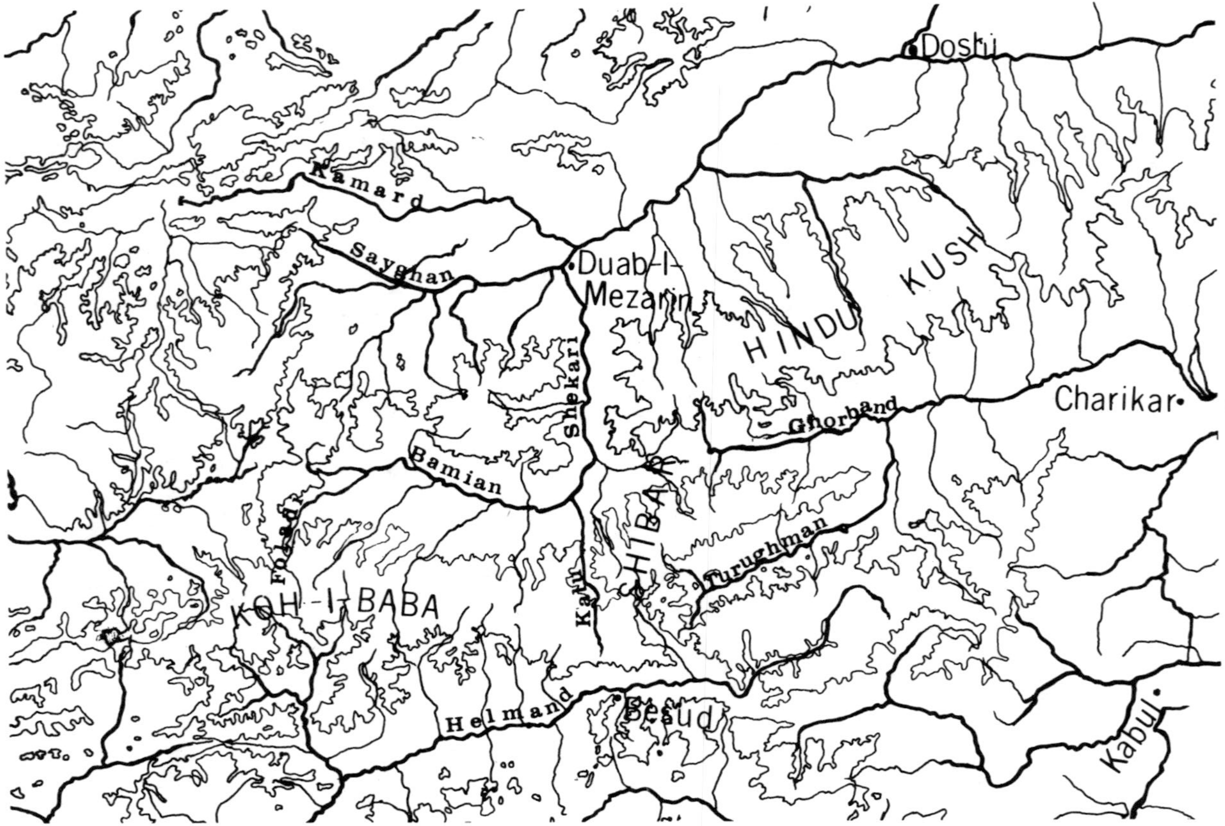


Figure 1. The east-central region of Afghanistan.

# I

# THE PROBLEM AND THE ISSUES

## THE SETTING

### The Spatial Setting

THIS study attempts to explain why three Islamic sects are distributed in a regular way across the landscape of Bamian, Afghanistan, and why the village communities of Shibar, its eastern part, have internally divided into opposing religious sects.

Afghanistan, like most of the countries of the Middle East and Soviet Central Asia, is a plural society, composed of several ethnic groups interrelating through the market and dominated by one of them (Furnival, 1948), the Afghans (=Pushtuns=Pathans). It is also plural in a religious sense, for it is primarily made up of three muslim sects–Sunnis, Imamis, and Ismailis–one of which, the Sunnis, predominates. Sunnis control the ruling institution and the strategic geographical regions of Afghanistan. In its southern and eastern parts, Afghan and Tajik Sunnis preponderate and in the north, Uzbek, Afghan, Tajik, and Hazara (Day Zainat) Sunnis are pre-eminent. The most numerous rural Imami groups are the Hazara-Sayyed Imamis dwelling in the inaccessible mountain massif of central Afghanistan, the Hazarajat, and the Tajik Imamis of Herat Province. The Ismaili sects[1] follow the contours of the Hindu Kush Mountain range from its southern extremity in Besud northeastward into the Pamirs, even into Russian Central Asia and Northern Pakistan.

Shibar, the eastern portion of Bamian, is part of the band of Ismaili-occupied territories. Shibar forms one of the more passable saddles over the great mountainous divide which parts the waters of Central Asia from those of South Asia. To the north of Shibar the mountain range is called the Hindu

[1] The Ismailis are here referred to as sects, in the plural, because the Ismailis toward the southern end of their territories pay respect to a different Saint than those of the northern end (those called in the ethnographic literature, "Mountain Tajiks") and because in certain minor respects their beliefs and practices are different, the southern type having renounced some years ago the veneration of Saints.

Kush; to its south and west, the Koh-i-Baba. East of the Shibar saddle is the Ghorband valley, whose waters, flowing east, join the Panjshir River in Koh-Daman and eventually the Kabul-Indus. Ghorband is a forty-mile-long defile, bounded by steep mountain slopes, whose rivulets water a fertile alluvial plain. Ghorband has one major tributary valley, the Turughman (or Turkman) valley, whose waters come off the ridge overlooking Shibar from the south. West of the Shibar saddle is the Bamian valley, whose waters, the Bamian River and its tributaries, are the extreme southern sources of the Qunduz-Oxus River that eventually debouches into the Aral Sea. North of Shibar is the southern extremity of the region dominated by the town of Duab-i-Mezarin and the city of Doshi. This region lies at the southern end of the greater Turkestan region presided over by the cities of Baghlan, Qunduz, and Khanabad, and further west, by Tashqurghan (formerly Khulm), Mazar-i-Sharif, and Balkh. The Baghlan-Qunduz-Khanabad region is washed by waters originating in Bamian, joined further down (i.e., to the north) by those of Sayghan, Kamard, and Andarab. South of Shibar, over the ridge that constitutes the eastern end of the Koh-i-Baba mountain, the land drains in two directions, eastward and westward. The valley of this ridge is the upper source of the Turughman River, a tributary of Ghorband. The valley west of it is Besud, whose waters are the upper sources of the Helmand River flowing southwest into the expansive Hamun-i-Helmand saline lake.

Shibar, therefore, lies near the sources of three great rivers of Central and South Asia, the Helmand, the Kabul-Indus and the Qunduz-Oxus. It also lies in a region marginal to the centers of political influence within Afghanistan. Administratively, the Bamian valley to the west of Shibar is now assigned to Bamian Province which includes the valleys of Sayghan and Kamard and the town of Duab-i-Mezarin to the north and the districts of Yak Awlang and Day Kundi to the west and southwest; the region surrounding Doshi due north of Shibar belongs to the Province of Baghlan; the valley of Ghorband to its east, to the Province of Parwan; and the valley of Besud to its south, to the Province of Maydan. Shibar itself is assigned to Bamian. This greater area, composed of the valleys surrounding Shibar—i.e., Bamian, Doshi, Ghorband, and Besud—are here referred to as the east-central region of Afghanistan. The highland ridge formed by the Shibar plateau, and the highlands of the Hindu Kush immediately north and east of it, are here called the southern Hindu Kush highlands.

This study is directly concerned with only a segment of the east-central region, the Bamian segment, of which Shibar forms the eastern ridge, but it appears to be representative of social conditions in the entire region. Society in the Shibar highlands is generally characteristic of its adjacent highlands, and society in the Bamian valley is more or less similar to the lowlands of Doshi, Ghorband, and Besud. Differences in the relationship of these areas to broader political influences will be explained later.

## The Cultural Setting

The populations of east-central Afghanistan are culturally divided into a number of distinct groups by several overlapping criteria: relation to the government, ecologic adaptations, patrilineal descent, and religious sect.

The criteria of relationship to the government and of ecological adaptation are the bases on which non-peasant and peasant populations are distinguished. Of the non-peasants, who are not the concern of this study, there are two kinds, government officials and nomads. The officials are appointed to government service by the ruling institution in Kabul. The capital for Bamian Province, which includes territories west and north as well as the valley itself, has been established at the town of Bamian in the heart of the valley. It is responsible for several subdistricts (*wuluswalis*), each of which may also have one or several rural stations (*alaqadaris*). Almost all government appointees at these installations are outsiders, but some local residents, usually rather prominent persons, have been appointed for lower echelon positions. A few teachers, all but one of them for the primary grades, and several clerks were appointees from among the local residents in 1968. Besides those appointed from Kabul a number of local residents are hired with government funds by the provincial officials to do menial tasks: guarding storerooms, caring for government-owned groves of trees, and the like. Generally even these positions confer some prestige upon a local resident, as it provides him with some personal acquaintance with government officials and of course a small cash salary.

The nomads are primarily adapted to a pastoral subsistence. Most of the pastoral nomads move through Ghorband and Bamian during the spring on their way to their summer pastures further west in central Afghanistan, and retrace their route in the fall on the way to winter pastures in the eastern provinces of Afghanistan. A few families of the smaller tribes move into the mountains of Bamian and Ghorband during the summer where the summer vegetation can support small numbers of their flocks as well as those owned by the local peasants. A very few nomad families encamp for the summer months on lands of the local peasants, usually in the better lowland regions, because through giving loans they have acquired more or less permanent liens on the peasants' properties and incomes. In rare cases nomad families have permanently settled on these lands themselves (Ferdinand, 1959, 1962). All of these nomads belong to the Afghan ethnic group and to the Sunni sect.[2]

The peasant agricultural populations, who are the subject of this study, are culturally grouped by patrilineal descent and Islamic sect. By patrilineal descent

[2] Besides the Afghan nomads there are a few families of Jats who come into the area during summer. Little is known about this ethnic group, even by most residents of Afghanistan (see Bataillard, 1843, 1875; Bray, 1925; Burton, 1851, 1898; Grierson, 1889).

they are grouped into several ethnic types: Tajiks, Afghans, Hazaras, Sayyeds, Afshars, Afghans, and Arabs.[3] Of these groups the most populous are the Tajiks and Hazaras. Sayyeds exist also in fair numbers, but except for their claim of descent from the Prophet, they are generally indistinguishable from Hazaras. Physically, the Hazaras are typically distinguishable from the Afghans and Tajiks by their Mongoloid features. The Imami Sayyeds, Afshars and Arabs, having intermarried with the Hazaras, commonly have Mongol features. Nevertheless, contrary to common belief, phenotype did not always seem to me a clearly distinguishable criterion of ethnic identity. Some Hazaras, especially those from the chiefly families, do not have clearly defined Mongoloid features. Instead, some have heavy beards and lack the typical Mongolian eyefolds and high cheek bones. Conversely, some persons calling themselves "Tajik" have rather strong Mongoloid features. I consequently doubt that the relationship between phenotype and ethnic identity is very close.

Religiously, the peasant populations are divided into Sunnis, Imamis, and Ismailis. Dogmatic differences not being a concern of this study, their theological orientations need only be briefly mentioned.[4] Sunnism, the early leaders of which were called the Califs of the Muslim community, is usually considered the orthodox sect. The Imamis and Ismailis are Shiite groups who broke from the "orthodox" (Sunni) Muslim community after the death of the fourth Calif, Ali. They recognize Ali and his descendants, whom they call Imams, as the only legitimate successor of the Prophet. There have been several kinds of Shiites. The Imamis are those who recognize twelve Imams, the last of whom has disappeared but is to reappear before the final judgment. The Imamis are sometimes called "Twelvers" and in Afghanistan are known by the Arabic equivalent, *Athna-Asharia.* The Ismailis recognize the first six Imams but differ with the Imamis over the subsequent line of succession. Subsequent to the sixth Imam, they follow a different line that continues to the present day, the present Imam being the Agha Khan.

Persons do not readily identify themselves as members of one sect or another. Instead, their sectarian membership is typically expressed in terms of their allegiance to a Saint whose sectarian loyalties are generally known. The Sunni populations of Bamian venerate different Sunni Saints, all of whom reside outside the east-central region. The Imamis venerate two Imami authorities, one in Yak Awlang and the other in Kabul. The Ismailis pay respect to a Sayyed residing in the highlands near Doshi.

There is a close correlation between ethnicity and sect affiliation. The ethnic categories "Tajik" and "Afghan" imply the sectarian category "Sunni";

[3]The cultural features of these groups are described in the literature. See Schurmann (1962) and Wilbur (1956) for a description of these groups. For more detail on the Hazaras see Bacon (1951*a*, 1951*b*, and 1958) and Ferdinand (1959).

[4]See Gibb et al., 1954 for more detail.

"Afshar" implies "Imami"; and "Hazara" and "Sayyed" imply either "Imami" or "Ismaili" religious affiliation. This correlation between ethnicity and sect identity is so close that when informants mentioned instances of Hazaras converting to Sunnism, they spoke of them as having "become Tajik." The Arabs, who live primarily by smithing, are an exception to this rule, for they belong to the sects of the communities in which they dwell.

There is a close correlation between spatial location, ethnicity, and sect affiliation. The strategic lowland centers are populated by the Sunni ethnic groups and the highlands by the Imami or Ismaili groups. Of the Sunni groups in the strategic lowlands, the Tajiks are the most numerous. In Bamian, Tajiks live on the central lowland plain and in valleys of Jalmish, Ghandak, Sayghan, and Kamand, which are north of the central valley. There are only a few Afghan villages in Bamian; they are located only in the lowlands, often on the fringe of the Tajik populations. The officials assigned to government offices in the strategic lowland centers of the region are almost entirely Sunnis; the few Imamis in government hold only low-echelon positions. The lowlands, then, are controlled by Sunnis: Sunni Tajiks, Sunni Afghans, and Sunni officials. The highlands are inhabited by the Imami or Ismaili Hazara-Sayyed populations. A few Afshar communities, always Imamis, dwell among the Imami Hazara-Sayyed communities, sometimes on the fringes of the lowlands, where the Hazara and Tajik lands meet. The highlands are therefore occupied by the Imami and Ismaili ethnic groups: Hazaras, Sayyeds, and Afshars.

## THE PROBLEM

The distribution of the religious sects in Bamian is the problem. Sunnis occupy the central valley of Bamian, Imamis the southern and western highlands, and a mixture of Imamis and Ismailis the highlands of Shibar and Kalu (see Fig. 2).

The most complex aspect of the problem is the mixture of sects in Shibar and Kalu, where sectarian lines cross-cut the numerous highland valleys and glens, forming among the populations a kind of chessboard of contrasting religious allegiances in which adjacent villages often belong to contrary sects. Even more remarkably, in Shibar (but not Kalu) the dividing line between the sects sometimes cuts through hamlet groups consisting of closely related agnatic kinsmen.

The valley of Labmushak in Shibar (Fig. 3) furnishes an example of the sectarian chessboard and the fractured hamlet groups. People in Labmushak are grouped in a number of small hamlets, each composed of closely related agnates and their families. Generally the members of each hamlet belong to the same sect. For example, inhabitants of Juraqol, Pesh Zyar and Qalaay-Mullah are all

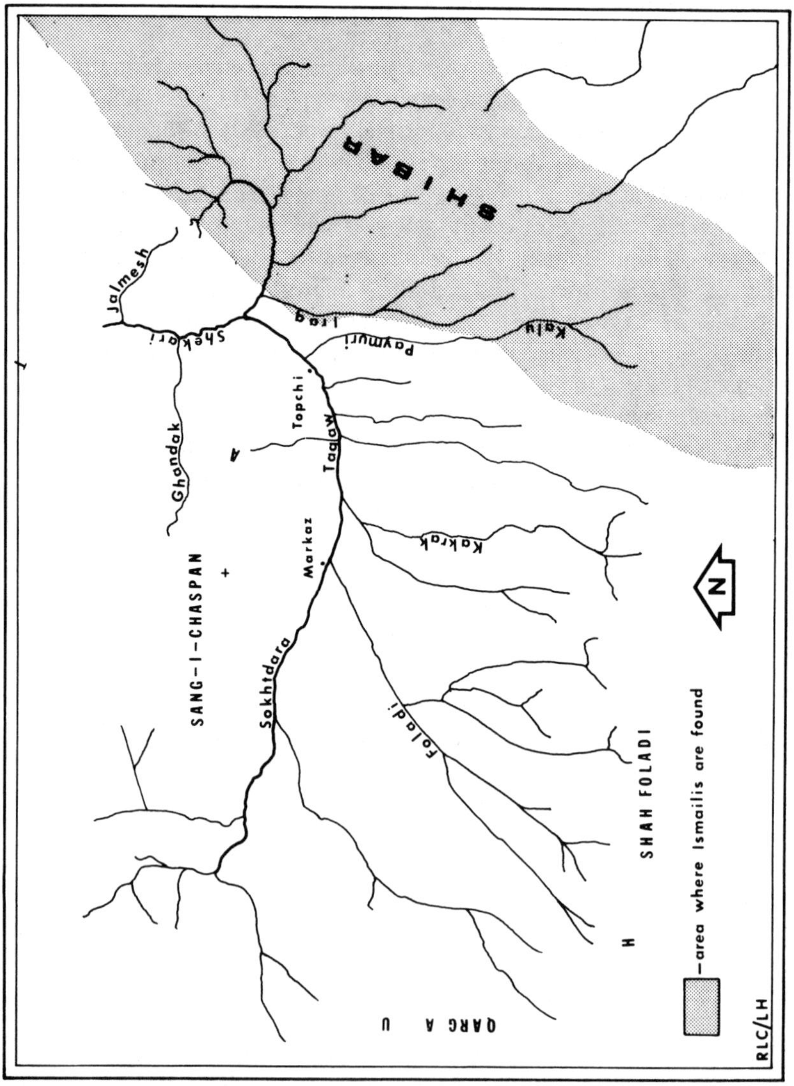


Figure 2. Locational map of Bamian

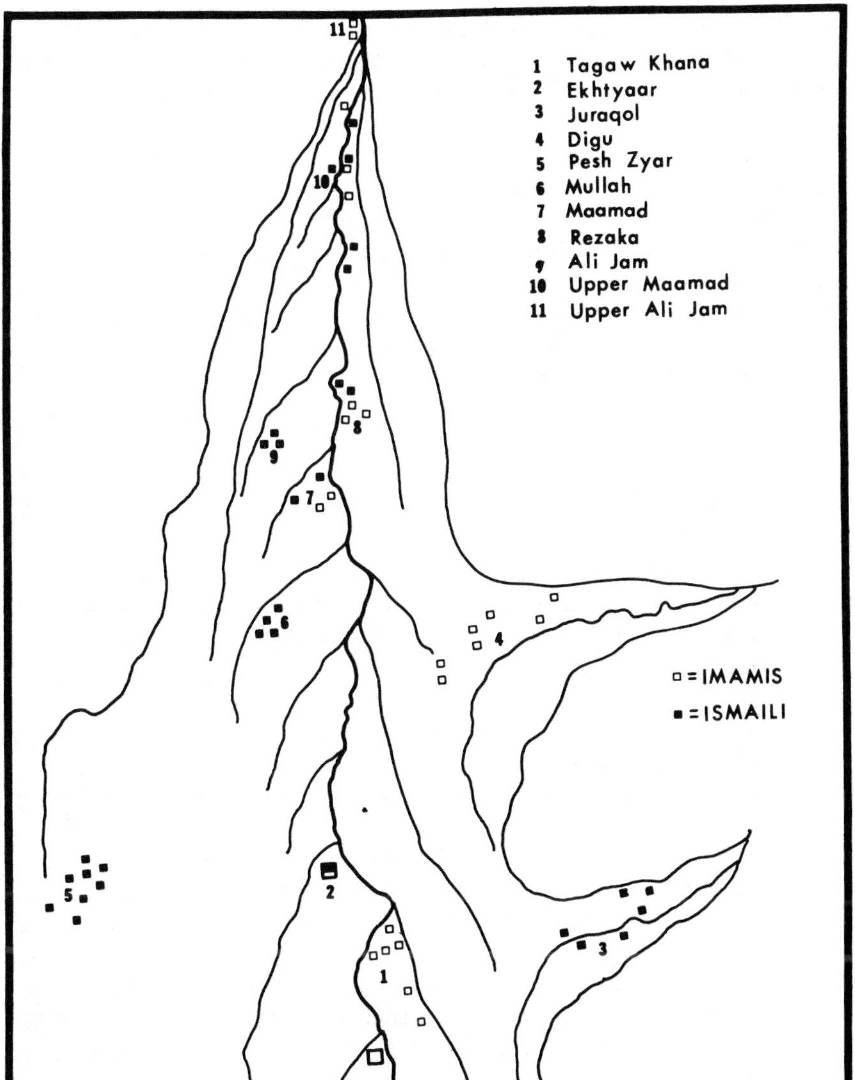


Figure 3. The distribution of sects in Labmushak

Ismailis, while the populations of Tagaw Khana and Digu are entirely Imamis. However, at three locations—Rezaka, Upper Maamad, and Ekhtyaar—where sectarian allegiances have cut through their kinship and territorial groupings, the distribution of sects is less regular. This pattern of social segmentation, in which some hamlets are broken and others not, exists in many valleys throughout the highlands of Shibar. And in most valleys of Shibar both sects are represented.

These religious differences are the overriding criteria of social segmentation in Afghanistan. The break between Ismailis and Imamis in Labmushak, even where it cuts through hamlet groups, represents the most significant cleavage in their society. Thus the inhabitants of this valley are actually divided into functioning groups that bear no apparent resemblance to their spatial arrangement or kinship connections.

The extent of sect group separation in Labmushak is indicated by the following facts:

1. They do not intermarry. Marriages are consummated between members of the same sects.
2. The Ismailis and Imamis reckon themselves to belong to different patrilineages, even though some of them obviously—*in casu* the broken hamlets—are closely related. A woman of Rezaka, for example, denied having any kinship ties with a neighboring family who had converted to the contrary sect.
3. They do not graze their sheep and goats in the same flocks; each flock is composed of animals owned by sect brothers.
4. Each sect group patronizes different water-powered flour mills. Six are Ismaili mills and three are Imami.
5. They patronize different occupational specialists. The Ismailis of Labmushak patronize two Ismaili brick masons, one in Juraqol and the other in an adjacent valley. The Imamis use the services of a brick mason residing in another valley. Thus, an Imami in Tagaw Khana makes a 45-minute walk to reach an Imami brick mason rather than patronize the Ismaili brick mason in nearby Juraqol. Similarly, two Arab ironsmiths reside in the valley, one in Pesh Zyar serving Ismailis, the other in Katyalaw serving Imamis.
6. Borrowing, lending, buying and selling of petty amounts of goods seldom cross sectarian lines. Ismailis trade with Ismailis within and outside the valley, and Imamis likewise trade only with Imamis. Trade with other internally broken valleys is carried on in parallel lines, but within the sects. Residents of Labmushak, for example, exchange their surplus alfalfa for pears produced in another valley, Alawlab, but as Alawlab is also divided, the transactions are carried on between sect brethren in the two valleys. When farmers search for extra straw or a loan of wheat

until harvest, they first contact members of their own sect. When they have to move further afield in search of goods, they may buy outside sectarian lines, but they stay overnight with members of their own sect.

7. Conversation between members of the two sects is short, to the point, and sometimes strained by attempts to veil information in vapid generalities. Sometimes remarks are downright hostile. Members of different sects, when passing on the mountain pathways, do not usually greet each other.

This pattern of isolation between the sects in Labmushak has not always been so severe. The degree of interaction has ebbed and flowed irregularly. There have been times when members of the two sects have spoken more freely; sometimes they have helped each other in common tasks and participated in major social events. There have occasionally been large wedding feasts which everyone in the area attended, as must have been the practice in former times. But when tensions develop the groups separate. A few years ago some Imami and Ismaili families were grazing their livestock together and relations between them seemed to be improving, but a bitter argument arose because an especially pietistic Imami elder, who was sponsoring a wedding feast, refused to accept an Ismaili person's gift of a lamb for his feast. This incident led to the severance of all social interaction between the two groups.

The chessboard of contrary religious alignments shows that individuals or groups have converted to one or the other sect and have remained in their home community alongside kinsmen adhering to the original sect. Nevertheless most people initially deny that conversion is possible. I was told the following, for example:

> If a man changes from one sect to another, he does not change from Imami to Sunni or from Sunni to Imami; he becomes an infidel but not anything else.
>
> If my brother became Imami my father and I would be furious, and the others also would not let him into their houses.
>
> A person can't change his religion. Never. The judge would be unhappy—no one could ever do this—and his Saint and his mullah would not accept it. People would reproach him for it; they would call him an apostate.
>
> It is not really feasible to change from one sect to another. A person cannot really get free from his sect. Suppose your Saint should say something unfriendly to you, would not be nice to you or should not be courteous to you; then you would have to go. If he looked badly toward you and refused to allow you to come see him, then you would be out. Then

suppose one day you have to find a friend. You couldn't find a friend in a whole year. If you fight with everybody, then in a single day you can become the enemy of everyone.

The problem may now be stated in four questions:

1. What conditions favor the distribution of the Sunni groups in the lowlands, the Imamis in the highlands, and the Ismailis in only the highlands of the southern Hindu Kush, of which Shibar is a part?
2. What conditions could have allowed communities to factionalize along sect lines in Shibar, but not elsewhere in Bamian?
3. How can religious conversion have taken place when conversion is said to be impossible?
4. What conditions induce these groups to formulate their factional differences—if they have to factionalize—as religious differences? Why are the factions conceived as religious sects?

## THE ISSUES

These questions are relatively unfamiliar to anthropologists and the solutions to be offered must be considered provisional. Nevertheless, the ethnographic material in this study is presented to support a more general thesis: that the sects of Bamian are political interest groups whose form and distribution are controlled by their social, cultural, and geographic contexts. The argument impinges on three issues of broad concern.

### The Geography of Discrete Social Units

It is not unusual that religious sects are distributed in a regular way in Bamian, for throughout the Middle East orthodox Islam prevails at the political and economic centers while various forms of heresy persist in the mountains (Coon, 1951; Planhol, 1959). Nevertheless, anthropologists have given little attention to the social processes bringing about such a pattern. Leach roughly tied the political structures of Kachin-Shan society to geographical contexts but as his problem was somewhat different ("how far it can be maintained that a single type of social structure prevails throughout the Kachin area" [1954:3]), he did not develop a clear-cut model of the relation between Kachin-Shan societies or *gomsa-gumlao* political structures and their geographic contexts. Barth (1956) has shown that the distribution of ethnic groups in Swat is regulated by the locations of specific ecologic niches exploited by different ethnic groups, and by the relative power balance between the groups competing within the same niche. Other authors (Sahlins, 1964; Harding, 1967; Irons, 1969; Wolf, 1956, 1966; Y. Cohen, 1969) have stressed that the social structure of groups should be related to their political as well as ecologic contexts.

Planhol (1959), a human geographer, has pointed out that in the Middle East religious minorities typically dwell in mountain or desert refuges apart from the great trade routes, or, if in the cities, maintain their isolation by economic specialization. This study similarly takes the view that religious heterodoxy in inaccessible rural areas of the Middle East is a boundary-maintaining device of interest groups dwelling in the marginal territories.

The factor of geographic marginality requires some explanation. The ability of a polity to impinge on other groups is limited by three factors: its relative power, its distance from the other groups, and the kinds of controls it seeks to impose on them. The first of these requires no explanation. The second, the effect of distance, is not to be understood as linear distance, but effective distance. The effective distance of a society from its neighbors is a consequence of its technological capabilities for crossing space and the costs and gains of economic exchange with its neighbors. As an example of the technological factors in effective distance, China's ability to control Tibet has increased as her technology has developed, from an earlier system of communication and transport based on oxcarts, riverboats, and camel caravans to a system based on railroads, aircraft, radios, and telephones. As an example of the economic factors in effective distance, some peasant communities of China's northern frontier once were tied more closely to the societies to their north than to certain much closer communities to the south. This was because camel transport across the Mongolian steppes was cheaper than oxcart transport southward to the city, and consequently the peasants found it more profitable to sell grain to Mongol pastoralists 800 miles to the north than to urban Chinese merchants scarcely one tenth of that distance to the south (Lattimore, 1956).

The third limit on a society's reach across space is the kind and degree of influence it attempts to exert on its neighbors. Lattimore (1956) has pointed out that a society can reach out comparatively farther by conquest than it can administratively or economically integrate marginally held territories into the central socio-economic system (see also Bailey, 1957).

These limitations on the range of a society's influence across space stablish its political and economic frontiers. The interest groups at its frontiers therefore may retain a degree of autonomy from it, formulated as contrastive social identities (Canfield, in press).

## The Cultural Identity of Discrete Social Units

But why is the functional autonomy of marginal interest groups formulated as contrasting sectarian identities? Recent work on ethnic groups provides some clues. Barth (1969*b*) has suggested that the ascription of ethnic differences should be analytically distinguished from the social processes supporting such distinctions. The emphasis on ascription as the critical feature of ethnic discreteness enables the social analyst to specify how groups maintain continuity even though their cultural inventories change, how they can interact without violating their boundaries, and how persons can seep through their boundaries without disrupting the categorical distinctiveness of the groups. The present approach differs from Barth's treatment of ethnic groups in that it takes sectarian identity rather than ethnicity as the basic, most general social identity in Bamian (cf. Barth, 1969*b*:13, 17). It is curious, in fact, that Barth, though citing tribe, caste, language group, region, and state (1969*b*:34) does not include religion as a possible basis of "ethnic" ascription. This study argues that tactical considerations have made sectarian identity the primary basis of group categorization in Bamian, and in Afghanistan as a whole.

What factors elevate one ascribed distinction above another? Two propositions appear to answer this question. First, the categories of group identity are defined in the sphere of intergroup relations. Barbara Ward (1965, 1966) has pointed out that there is a correspondence between a group's conception of the identities of other societies and its conceptions of its own identity: the members of a group tend to see themselves in terms that are complementary to the diagnostic features of neighboring groups. Anthropomorphically speaking, a society is constantly asking questions about its identity in relation to its neighbors: "Who are we?" "What shall we be known by—as friends, kinsmen, trading partners, or enemies of our neighbors?" "How are we different from them?"

The sets of answers to such questions invoked by each society result in the "mosaics" of different social groups on the landscape, the discrete groups of persons who feel they belong together vis-a-vis other groups. Through such means other groups are identified as outsiders, whether they are ensconced across the valley, over the mountain, or beyond the sea. By "viewing space through a screen of symbols" each group sees its social position among the spatially juxtaposed communities on the face of the land and maintains a structural pose consistent with that context (Geertz, 1965; Sahlins, 1964).

The second proposition is that the categories of group identity are generally controlled by the terms a dominant group uses to identify itself. The interest groups within its spheres of influence must conform to such requirements, either by ascribing to themselves an identity indicating their adherence to the dominant group, or by ascribing to themselves a different, complementarily opposite identity so as to pose themselves against it.

The Kau Sai exemplify the first stance, the Berbers of the Maghrib and the Hausa of Ibadan, the second. The people of Kau Sai have several "conscious models," or cultural conceptions, of what Chinese society is, one of which, their "immediate model" (i.e., their conception of themselves), is constructed after their conception of Chinese literati society. Their conception of literati society

> acts for them as their measure of what is truly Chinese, and wherever it is relevant, it is, and has been, used as a *corrective for their immediate model* [i.e., of themselves] *and so for their actual structure* (Ward, 1965:135; emphasis added).

The Kau Sai have identified with "Chineseness" and therefore in constructing their model of their own cultural identity have shaped an image, albeit imperfectly, that sought to approximate their conception of Chinese literati society.

The Berbers of Algeria and the Hausa of Ibadan have formulated their cultural identities so as to contrast with, rather than conform to, the identities of their neighbors. They, of course, are not so dominated by neighboring societies as the Kau Sai are by Chinese literati society. Rather than being eager to be identified with neighboring groups, they are careful to maintain their distinct cultural identities as "walls" partitioning their groups from those around them. To maintain such discreteness they have had to adjust the categories by which they remain apart from the others.

Several times, for instance, the mountain-dwelling Berbers have reformulated their religious identities in order to remain distinct from the polities controlling the lowland centers of power. These Berbers have almost always been religious heretics–viewing them of course from the perspective of their neighbors. When the Romans who controlled the province of Ifriqiya became Christianized, the highland Berbers (whom they never fully subjugated) also became Christians–but Donatist and Arian heretics, so as to remain distinct from the church of Rome. When Islam swept the area the Berbers became Muslims, but soon expressed their dissent from the inequalities of Arab Muslim rule by becoming Kharijite heretics. Even after this, their internecine divisions led to the formation of sectarian differences among themselves.

> The clearest indication that religious doctrine little concerned them fundamentally is given by the fact that one party espoused the cause of the Shiis, not only that of the Idrisids of Fas, but even of those who had come under the influence of the Persian outlook and saw in the *imam* an incarnation of the Divinity. Thus it came about that alongside the Kharidjis (Sufris and Ibadis) there were the Fatimids [Ismailis] (Basset and Pellat, 1960: 178).

The Hausa of Ibadan furnish a similar example, but in an urban context. When changes on the national level threatened to abolish the ethnic distinctions which had set them apart from the Yoruba groups and to undermine their monopoly of a lucrative trade network, they converted to an uncommon sect of Islam (A. Cohen, 1969).

The factors, then, that generally elevate certain ascriptive categories above others are inherent in the overarching socio-political context. A group that identifies with a neighboring group ascribes to itself an identity similar to that of its neighbor. A group that endeavors to remain distinct from its neighbors ascribes to itself a plainly contrary identity.

## The Crossing of Discrete Social Boundaries

Where such a boundary exists, how could an individual slip across it? There have been few anthropological studies of boundary crossing (see Barrett, 1968; Barth, 1969*a*; A. Cohen, 1969; Haaland, 1969; Sangree, 1966). In the societies studied, the categorical distinctions between groups have not been intensified by profound hostilities such as exist between sect groups in Bamian. The issue in this study is how conversion can take place between mutually hostile groups. To deal with such an issue a distinction must be made, already implicit in the other studies of boundary crossing, between the tactical and symbolic aspects of behavior. Tactical aspects of behavior are those resulting from the actor's rational assessment of the risks and opportunities involved in his behavior. A person manages and manipulates situations so as to achieve consciously conceived objectives.[5]

Symbolic or communicative aspects of behavior are those indicating the actor's relationship to the cultural ideals and categories of his society. In this sense all human social behavior, as it takes place within culturally conceived frameworks of meaning, is symbolic.

> A socially accepted system of ideas is imminent in every overt process of social interaction, a system of ideas which in a quite literal sense informs it (Geertz, 1965:203).

For humans, social action is communicative action. Thus, a person's conformity to the standards of his society symbolizes his willingness to remain in fellowship with its other conforming members. His studied deviance from such standards, on the other hand, symbolizes his dissent from it, his unwillingness to remain in accord with it. Seen in this light, human behavior is a language of fellowship and conformity, and of dissent and resistance.

Neither the "tactical" nor the "symbolic" aspect of human behavior necessarily portrays the emotional sentiments of the actors. Their feelings are subject to the structural demands of their society in the sense that social conformity requires that animosities, if there be any, must be checked or veiled in order to

[5] See Alland (1967:212); Barth (1959); Bennett (1969*a*).

preserve social interaction and an appearance of solidarity.[6] Personal feelings of hostility, of course, sometimes do come to the surface. When they do, the functional bonds that hold persons together can be broken and even the pretense of unity among community members can be discarded. In such cases new patterns of behavior will appear and new conceptions of their identities will be formulated.

It is in such a context that persons cross the boundaries between mutually hostile groups. We shall argue that religious conversion is an option to defeated disputants in Shibar, but not elsewhere in Bamian, because ecological and political constraints on Shibar society allow a disputant to withdraw from his kinsmen without leaving his vital resource, irrigated land.

[6] Cf. Bennett (1969*a*:291-292) on "water fights" between persons who otherwise cooperate in economic activities.

# II

# CULTURAL ECOLOGY

## TOPOGRAPHY AND CLIMATE

### Topography and Population Distribution

BAMIAN has been referred to as a valley, as it is the region through which a river flows. Topographically, however, it has the appearance of a basin, though a crack to the northeast allows drainage to flow outside. It is shaped like an oblong bowl, the bottom of which is an alluvial valley, while its rim, irregular in height and thickness, is formed by mountain ridges and plateaus. From rim to rim it measures about 60 miles from east to west and 20 miles from north to south, but its central alluvial floor, known as Tagaw, is hardly ten and one-half miles long and at its widest point barely a mile broad.

The northern rim of the bowl is a row of immense sheer cliffs, rising in places over 300 feet above the valley floor. From east to west these cliffs become shallower and in places less abrupt. Behind them ascends the Koh-i-Khoja Ghar mountain which at the Sang-i-Chaspan Peak stretches to about 13,000 feet, almost 6,000 feet above the basin floor. Little water flows into the basin from this northern ridge; instead, the bulk of the moisture from these peaks drains northward into Ghandak and Sayghan. The southern ridge of the bowl ascends more gradually but at its highest point reaches nearly 17,000 feet. This is the Shah Foladi mountain range. Flowing northward off Shah Foladi into the Bamian valley, a number of streams water fertile highland valleys before disgorging onto the plain. The Shah Foladi and Koh-i-Khoja Ghar ridges run parallel to each other to form, respectively, the southern and northern rims of the basin. They are joined together at either end by the undulating plateaus of Qarghanatu on the west and Shibar on the east. The Qarghanatu plateau is the watershed between the Bamian and Band-i-Amir rivers. Shibar, of course, is the watershed between Bamian and Ghorband. The eastward-flowing waters of Tagaw, at their confluence with a smaller stream from Shibar, veers to the north and–surging with great force through Shekari Gorge, an immense cleft in the northern ridge of the basin, sometimes as narrow as 50 feet–disgorges onto the plain of Afghan Turkestan whence it flows into the Qunduz river. The eastern half of Bamian gives the appearance of extreme ruggedness, cliffs rising in many places quite perpendicular to the valley floor, gorges often pinching the valleys into isolated, elongated segments of cultivation alongside the path of the river. The undulations, however, of the western half become milder, but rise higher than the eastern plateau.

The settled populations are entirely distributed alongside the rivers and streams of the basin. The most populous region is the Tagaw plain itself. Tagaw's expansive western end, where the mouths of the Foladi, Sokhtdara, and Kakrak rivers converge, is the political nave of the basin. This area is known as the *markaz*, the "center," or as "Bamian" in its narrowest sense, for from this area the entire province has been named. Extensive archaeological remains witness to its ancient political importance; even today the present provincial headquarters of the Afghan government are situated on a plateau overlooking the markaz. The eastern end of Tagaw and an expansive tributary valley, Paymuri, form another population node where the remains of Shahr-i-Zohak, "The Red City," also testify to the historic importance of this location. Most of the other tributary valleys of Tagaw are economically and socially less closely linked to Tagaw because they are essentially cut off from it by the convoluted terrain. These valleys, situated high among the rugged plateaus surrounding Tagaw, provide sanctuary for additional populations which, taken altogether, exceed the number dwelling on Tagaw.

Bamian's populations are spatially divided into two groups, those associated with Tagaw and those associated with the isolated highland valleys. The populations of Tagaw are spatially clustered; those in the highlands are pocketed in relatively small groups. Each village and territory is named, and since territorial location is closely associated with social identity, one's home territory usually defines one's social identity.

## Climate

Statistics on temperature and precipitation have only recently been systematically recorded. Generally, the plain of Tagaw, being somewhat higher than Kabul, is a few degrees colder. The British in 1840 recorded a February temperature of -10 to -12 degrees (Fahrenheit) for several nights at the markaz (Government of India, 1910:11). During one May day in 1967 temperatures on the plain ranged from a low of 37 degrees to a high of 72 degrees (Fahrenheit). July-August is the warmest time of the year: temperatures rise to 90 degrees or more in the sun, but shade is always comfortable.

Summer precipitation is light, most of it falling on the eastern plateaus where the final dregs of moisture in the monsoon winds from South Asia are squeezed out of the atmosphere. The western plateau, owing to the dryness of the summer winds reaching it, is comparatively arid.

Winter winds pass from the other direction across the basin depositing most of the basin's precipitation in the form of snow. As a result of Tagaw's location on the southern (and warmer) side of Koh-i-Khoja Ghar and the sheltering affects of the abrupt cliffs overlooking Tagaw, it has a considerably more temperate climate in winter, though still cold, than its mountainous perimeters, where the snow descends in great quantities. Tagaw and some of its tributary valleys often get no more than a foot or two of snow in winter; the highland plateaus are generally blanketed with deep snow, tons of it heaved by powerful winds into immense drifts. Consequently, the inhabitants of the peripheral plateaus are forced to stay indoors several weeks during winter. Due to the extreme temperatures, the animals are kept inside the houses on the ground floor while the people hibernate in small groups around kitchen fires on the second story. Human transport in winter is extremely difficult, further thwarted by the wolves prowling close among the human habitations. Massive piles of fuel bushes reveal the severity of this environment. Farmers frequently spend 50 to 60 half-days a year collecting for fuel the bushes that grow on the barren crags and rock slides presiding over their fields. For nearly as many days of summer the women are occupied with preparing dung cakes for winter fuel.

The Bamian basin on a whole, therefore, presents an image of geographic isolation. Until recently, since a government snow plow has begun to keep the Shibar pass open for transport most of winter, all the passes into Bamian were practically closed during cold seasons. The journal of Charles Masson (1842, vol. II:459-64) describes the perils of crossing the snowbound passes of Bamian in winter.

There is a differential, however, in the degree to which the populations of Bamian are isolated. Bamian's strategic location along the main trade routes between India and Balkh have enabled the people at Bamian's central nave on Tagaw to retain contact, even in winter, with the outside world through the persistent flow of caravans over its passes and into its milder lowlands, where all paths converge. In contrast, the severity of winters on the surrounding plateaus of the basin still isolate the local inhabitants from one another and the outside world for several weeks, even for as long as three months, of the year. This isolation is greatest in the eastern flank of the Koh-i-Baba, notably in Kalu and Shibar where the snows are especially extensive and where the valleys do not directly lead into the Tagaw plain. The word *kohband*, "mountain bound," describes the social as well as geographic implications of life in such mountain communities, for it connotes social backwardness and religious conservatism and prudishness. People of Shibar report that until 10 to 12 years ago they frowned on association with urbanites and were extremely critical of life in Kabul. This point of view contrasts with that of the inhabitants of Tagaw who have for centuries been in regular contact with the populations of Kabul and Koh-Daman and have identified with urban centers outside Bamian. This has been especially true of the populations dwelling near the markaz, where the trade route between Kabul and Afghan Turkestan has long been an important source of economic gain.

## ECONOMIC ADAPTATIONS

### Economic Activities

Three kinds of economic activities are carried on in the basin, usually in combination: agriculture, animal husbandry, and commerce. Cultivation of the soil is the most important. Grain crops for subsistence are raised throughout the basin; a few cash crops are raised on the Tagaw. The subsistence grain crops are wheat, barley, and fava bean (*baqoli*).[1] Wheat is grown wherever possible, and barley where the land is worn out or has only a short growing season. Fava bean, though not a grain in the botanical sense, functions as an alternative to wheat and barley, for it is raised on irrigated soil in rotation with wheat in places where the growing season is long and surface water abundant, and it is ground up into flour and mixed (usually) with wheat and (sometimes) barley flour.

Crop raising for cash is a relatively new development in Bamian. The cash crops are mainly potatoes and trees. Potatoes are raised by a few families on the markaz, but the practice seems to be spreading upwards into the lower regions of Foladi valley. Presumably the cultivation of potatoes will spread even further up the warmer tributaries of the Tagaw plain.

Poplar trees are raised for sale as roofing beams for the adobe brick structures used in many places in Afghanistan. Large groves of poplar trees exist on Tagaw, owned by the rich and the Afghan government, and small groves are found in warmer parts of the highlands, usually on mountain slopes too rugged and rocky for plowing. In the highest valleys trees are relatively scarce. Poplar trees have only been cultivated for a few years. Elderly persons remember when trees were practically non-existent in many parts of the basin. But the demand for building materials in Kabul has made poplar trees increasingly profitable.

A few other products of Bamian are produced for cash. Eggs are sold by a few peasants to merchants on the markaz and shipped to Kabul. On the Qarghanatu plateau small amounts of peas, which grow acceptably in dry regions, are raised for cash. A dried form of yogurt (*qurut*) is also sold to markaz merchants by the peasants of the western portion of Bamian.

Husbandry of sheep and goats is carried on mainly as a supplement to cultivation. It is most feasible for the populations dwelling near enough to the highland pastures to bring their flocks home from pasture each night. Most of the highland populations keep flocks in numbers consonant with local conditions of

[1] *Vicia Faba L.* (Vavilov and Bukinich, 1929).

pasturage and capability for protection in winter. They are limited in the amount of grazing stock they can keep by the severe winters, requiring the livestock to be kept indoors for several months of the year. They are also limited in their right to graze their flocks because in the last century a concession of mountain grazing rights was given by the ruler of Kabul to the Pushtun nomads who assisted him in conquering this territory. Even so, the abundance of wild grasses blanketing the mountain slopes in summer, though mainly consumed by the Pushtun nomads, is sufficient to enable the sedentary inhabitants of the basin to keep a few sheep and goats of their own, usually no more than 10 sheep and goats per household. The flocks in Qarghanatu and Foladi, however, are generally larger than those further east because pasturage on the western plateaus is more abundant.

The importance of flock grazing among the highlanders is indicated by the summer migrations of their families to the grassy elevated glens of the mountains. These mountain quarters are known as their *aylaq* (or *sarqol*). During summer the women and children move up into these aylaq lands to facilitate the grazing of flocks on the mountain pastures while the men spend most of their time on the irrigated lands below. The men visit the aylaq once or twice a week depending on its accessibility.

Commerce is an important activity for some of the wealthier families dwelling on the Tagaw plain, mainly those around the markaz. On the markaz there is a small market consisting of two rows of buildings on either side of the main road, which is the focus of the influx of manufactured goods from Kabul and salt from Khanabad. It is also the center for the export of locally produced agricultural products to Kabul and Charikar to the east, and Pul-i-Khumri, Khanabad, and Mazar-i-Sharif to the north. The main products shipped out are wheat, dried yogurt (qurut), eggs, potatoes, and trees.

The merchants of this market are mostly from families locally resident at the markaz. Such families, besides having a member in charge of cultivating family lands, will have some members occupied in activities relating to the commercial market. These persons are owners of trucks or buses running to the urban centers, or drivers of vehicles moving in and out of the market, or shippers to the urban markets (where usually other family members are responsible for marketing their products), or shop owners vending the manufactured products brought in from the outside.

## Environmental Variables Affecting Agriculture

The crops of Bamian are planted in combinations according to the specific agricultural possibilities of each tillable tract of land. The following environmental variables affect the productive capacity of a piece of land: its altitude, its shading, the amount of surface water available to it, and the amount of precipitation on it. The first two of these variables affect its growing season, and the second two affect the mode of agricultural production.

*Altitude.* The irregular topography of most of Bamian is especially significant for agriculture, because the altitude of plots and the amount of their exposure to the sun vary widely enough to effect a multiplicity of ecological zones within a small area (see Porter, 1965). The lower a cultivated tract of land is, the more it benefits from warmer temperatures and from a longer growing season. Thus, the farmers of lowland plots have more certain yields and usually more latitude in the choice of crops than is possible for the highland farmers.

Among the highlands there is often a great deal of variation in the altitude of the alluvial floors within a single valley. The gradual rise in an alluvial floor places each cultivated plot in the valley at a slightly different altitude. In the distance of a mile a plain may ascend as much as 1500 feet, and thus compress the seasonal variations affected by altitude into a very short space.

*Shade.* Mountain ridges often shade different portions of a valley unevenly with the result that some cultivated lands, shaded early or late in the day (sometimes both early and late), have noticeably shorter growing seasons than those more exposed to the sunlight. This shading of the cultivated plains by the mountains and cliffs materially affects the growing seasons of the plots because of the generally high altitudes in Bamian. This effect is indeed much more apparent in the highlands where the contrast in the temperature of directly sunlit areas and shaded areas is greatest, and where a greater percentage of the alluvial lands are shaded. Moreover, it is more pronounced in the eastern portion of the basin than the western because the softer convolutions of the western plateaus are seldom abrupt enough to shade the cultivated valleys.

The positions of a valley with respect to the sun of course affects the degree to which its steep slopes will actually shade it. Since the sun traverses the sky from east to west, a valley running east and west (such as Tagaw and a few smaller valleys, e.g., Bulola, Kamard, and Sayghan) gets more sun, more warmth, and as a result a longer growing season than a highly walled valley running north and south. Most of the valleys on the south and southeast of the basin are of the latter type and therefore are more susceptible to shading.

*Availability of surface water.* The amount and seasonal patterns of the rivers draining a valley determine, of course, how much water can be used for irrigation in a valley. Generally Bamian waters, supplied by the extensive snows of Koh-i-Baba and its spurs, is abundant. The Foladi River, Tagaw's biggest tributary, issues from giant moraine lakes situated high on the Shah Foladi mountain. These resources, joined by other rivers disgorging on the Tagaw plain, are more than enough to ensure Tagaw—long and comparatively wide as it is—with plenty of water for irrigation in summer when it is most needed. A few highland areas, in fact, notably Kalu, suffer from an over-abundance of water, for despite the rather steep decline of the irrigable plain, an abundance of mountain springs keeps its soils, even in the higher glens, rather too moist for optimal cultivation.

The exceptions to this general pattern of sufficient water occur in certain portions of the basin among the highest, narrowest valleys around the fringe of the basin, where the snows immediately above them may melt away before the summer heat is spent. It is in these small, narrow, highest valleys that water is used by turns and where spring water, if available, is dammed up for use when the vital stream has diminished to a trickle. Such communities obviously suffer disadvantages in the practice of irrigation agriculture.

*Amount and periods of precipitation.* The amount of precipitation on a piece of land is, of course, a critical factor determining whether the land can be profitably cultivated without irrigation. Winter snowfall brings to the soil the fertilizing benefits of nitrogen, while spring rains, in addition, provide timely moisture for summer growth. The eastern plateaus are the most favored regions of the basin in this respect, as they draw heavy snows in winter and the greatest amount of rain, slight though it sometimes is, in summer. The western margin of the basin toward Qarghanatu differs from the eastern in that it generally gets almost no rain in summer, though a lot of snow in winter. The result is a reduction in the feasibility of the Qarghanatu highlands for dry-land agriculture.

The benefits of rainfall, which is favorable for dry-land cultivation, therefore, may be considered in complementary distribution with the benefits of low altitude. In the low altitudes of Tagaw, where the climate is mildest, the advantages of irrigation agriculture are greatest; in the high altitudes of Shibar where the climate is more severe, the advantages of dry-land agriculture are greatest. The greatest contrast, therefore, in the agricultural adaptations of Bamian's settled populations is between Tagaw and Shibar. The social correlates of this ecological contrast are one of the central concerns of this study.

## Types of Agricultural Land

There are three types of agricultural land in Bamian: irrigated land, rainfall land, and cold spring-watered land. Irrigated land (*abi*) exists alongside the courses of rivers and streams. The entire Tagaw, being flat and well watered, is irrigated. The valleys marginal to the Tagaw, more irregular in form, are irrigated wherever alluvial fills allow. The irrigation ditches (*juys*) that supply these lands are all relatively small. Each appears to have been built by the local community using it. Although large-scale canal works (*nahar*) seem never to have existed in the basin, there are evidences that these smaller ditches have been in existence since ancient times. They typically fan out from the natural water sources, staying above the gently sloping plains onto which they eventually are released. From the air the irrigation system therefore somewhat resembles a great centipede, its myriad legs (the ditches) fanning out from its body (the natural stream) at successively lower levels down each irrigated valley (see Fig. 3). As the legs represent specific elevations at which the water is being held above the plain, they outline the contours of the hills demarcating the edges of the plain. Where the hills are steep the legs cluster together one above another around the edge of the plain; where hills slope more gently the legs fan out more widely. And of course where the hills are too abrupt there may be no legs at all. Usually the land between the legs is irrigated, but sometimes on the edges of the plains there are patches of uncultivable land below the ditches due to the steepness of the slope; eventually the water lines reach the more gently sloping plateaus which they were built to serve. All the alluvial plains of the basin are irrigated except for a few on the southern edge of Koh-i-Khoja Ghar where the absence of a year-round flow of water and the frequency of flash floods combine to prevent cultivation.

The edges of the irrigated zone may be gradually creeping higher, for a few square yards of new land seem to be opened to irrigation each year. Because the only lands available for extending irrigation cultivation are the rugged steep banks of the hill above the alluvial floors, only small amounts of new land, with great effort, can be brought under cultivation each year. Opening up new irrigated land involves not only new construction or the extension of a canal, but also the clearing of land to be irrigated. Work on a ditch requires group help, but the clearing of each plot to be irrigated is the responsibility of the individual owner.

Some land receives enough rainfall to be cultivable without irrigation. Rainfall lands (*lalmi*) often also receive heavy snowfalls in winter and are consequently kept relatively fertile. Being very high, they have relatively short growing seasons and their crops are sometimes ruined by unseasonably early frosts. In Qarghanatu there are some poorly watered, problematic rainfall lands; but the best rainfall lands are in Shibar where rainfall, particularly on its highest slopes, is plentiful enough to ensure regular crops. Rainfall land, therefore, is especially valuable in Shibar.

Within Shibar, there is a continuum in the relative importance of rainfall agriculture. The higher (i.e., the more easterly) lands receive the most rainfall. They are rolling slopes, less steep and rocky than lower down toward the center of the basin, and consequently are more easily plowed. Moreover, most of them are in easy view of their owner's dwellings and thus are more easily protected from wild fauna or carelessly watched flocks. Further down in the basin, however, where rugged cliffs and gorges form, the reduced precipitation, the rockiness, steepness and inaccessibility of the cultivable dry lands combine to render rainfall agriculture less vital to subsistence.

Spring-watered tracts of land in some highland glens provide another kind of tillable land which is called simply *sarad* ("cold") land. Sarad land is different from rainfall land in that it is well watered by perennial springs. Indeed often it is too well watered, and has to be planted with vegetation that is not spoiled by a water surfeit. It is plowed and seeded, then left alone without much attention. It is similar to rainfall land in that it has only a short growing season, and may be spoiled by grazing animals and wild fauna. Sarad lands exist in different places in the Bamian highlands, but most extensively in Kalu, which, unlike Shibar, has almost no rainfall land. Sarad land is always used for supplementary agriculture.

## Ecologic Regions

The Bamian basin can be divided into six ecologic regions on the basis of the kinds of agricultural possibilities in each (see Table 1): the Tagaw plain, Khoja-Ghar Mountain, Shibar, Kalu, the Shah Foladi highlands, and Qarghanatu. The Tagaw region (Zone I) has numerous advantages. Low altitude (6800 feet) and an east-west orientation combine to provide the longest growing season in the basin; and abundant natural surface waters assure it of moisture necessary for irrigation. But it does not have the benefits of spring and summer rains. Winter snows are moderate.

Khoja-Ghar mountain (Zone II), owing to its ruggedness, has the fewest possibilities for land use. Very little of its southern slopes and cliffs is really usable. On some plateaus above the cliffs there is some spring vegetation useful for grazing. Only in a few places does water flow southward off this ridge, so there are few communities on its southern skirts. Many of these are located close to the Tagaw plain and also own land on Tagaw.

The valleys of Shibar (Zone III) are high, ranging in altitude from about 7500 to about 9500 feet, and most of them are north-south oriented. Generally, therefore, they have relatively short growing seasons, though the comparatively warm valley of Iraq is an exception. Surface water is abundant in most parts of Shibar except in those highest on the mountains. Fortunately, however, spring and summer rains fall, rendering rainfall agriculture possible on many unirrigable lands, complementing the irrigation agriculture. Moreover, in some places rain-watered lands particularly favor the highest valleys (where surface water is scarce) because the higher slopes receive the most rainfall. Winter snows are heavy, enhancing rainfall agriculture by fertilizing the soil.

The valley of Kalu (Zone IV), though north-south oriented, is wide and its hilly boundaries are not so abrupt as to shade much land. It is high, however, about the same altitude as the Shibar valleys, and therefore has a relatively short growing season. The numerous springs in the highest slopes above Kalu provide, as mentioned earlier, too much surface water, but there is little rainfall. Winter snows are heavy.

The valleys in the Shah Foladi highlands (Zone V) range in altitude from 7,500 to perhaps 10,500 feet above sea level. Often they are narrow and their hilly boundaries steep. Growing seasons therefore in these valleys are relatively short, especially short, of course, among those highest on the mountain. Surface water is generally sufficient except, again, in the highest valleys, but summer rainfall is minimal. Snows are relatively heavy but less than in Shibar.

TABLE 1

ECOLOGIC ZONES IN BAMIAN BASIN

| Zone Name | Topography | Altitude (ft.) | Orientation of Valleys to Sun | Growing Season | Winter Precipitation |
|---|---|---|---|---|---|
| I. Tagaw | wide, level plain bounded by cliffs, abrupt slopes | plain: 6,800 | east-west | long | moderate |
| II. Khoja-Ghar mountain | rugged | peak: 13,000 | north-south | none | moderate-heavy |
| III. Shibar | undulating plateaus, abrupt slopes, cliffs bounding narrow valleys | pass: 9,800<br>valleys: 8,000-9,500 | north-south | short | heavy |
| IV. Kalu | wide, undulating plain, shallow slopes and cliffs bounding wide plain | pass: 10,000<br>valleys: 8,000-9,500 | north-south | short | heavy |
| V. Shah Foladi | high mountain slopes, and some cliffs bounding narrow valleys | peak: 16,000<br>valleys: 8,000-10,500 | north-south | short | heavy |
| VI. Qarghanatu | undulating plateaus, shallow ravines | pass: 11,000<br>8,000-10,500 | north-south | short | heavy |

TABLE 1–*Continued*

| Summer Precipitation | Amount Surface Water | Accessible Summer Pasture | Land Uses | Means of Livelihood |
|---|---|---|---|---|
| very slight | abundant | none | irrig. agric. | subsistence activities: irrig. agric. cash activities: trees, potatoes; marketing |
| unknown | little or none | little or none | none | none |
| moderate-slight | adequate to (rarely) barely sufficient | abundant | Primary: irrig. agric.; rainfall agric. Secondary: pasture | subsistence activities: irrig. agric.; rainfall agric.; flock care cash activities: trees (few) |
| slight | too much | abundant | Primary: irrig. agric. Secondary: sarad agric.; pasture | subsistence activities: irrig. agric.; flock care |
| slight | adequate to (rarely) barely sufficient | abundant | Primary: irrig. agric. Secondary: pasture | subsistence activities: irrig. agric.; flock care; cash activities: trees (few) |
| slight | usually insufficient | abundant | Primary: irrig. agric. Secondary: (some) rainfall agric.; pasture | subsistence activities: irrig. agric.; flock care cash activities: peas |

The valleys of the Qarghanatu plateau on the western rim of Bamian (Zone VI) are about equally as high as those of the Shah Foladi highlands but the gentler slopes bounding them shade them less, and surface waters in late summer are less certain. There is, however, a limited amount of rainfall in the plateau and snows are rather heavy.

The land in each ecologic zone is used differently according to its natural possibilities. Everywhere in the basin (except Khoja Ghar), the primary economic use of the land is for irrigation agriculture. In Tagaw irrigation agriculture is the only use made of land. The other zones in the basin, however, have other kinds of land available. Pasture land is available to all the highland regions. In addition, rainfall land is abundant in Shibar. Sarad land is available in Kalu; and some rainfall land is available in Qarghanatu.

Everywhere in the basin subsistence irrigation agriculture is the vital economic adaptation; however, the supplementary means of livelihood differ according to the possibilities in each region. In Tagaw large amounts of potatoes and trees are raised for cash and, especially on the markaz, commercial activities are carried on. Everywhere else in the basin, with the exception of a little cashcropping in Qarghanatu, irrigation cultivation is supplemented by other activities for subsistence. In Shibar, irrigation is supplemented by rainfall agriculture and animal husbandry; in Kalu by sarad agriculture and flock care; in the Shah Foladi highlands by flock care; and in Qarghanatu by rainfall agriculture, some of the crop sold for cash, and by flock care.

As mentioned earlier, the contrast between Tagaw and Shibar is complementary. While Tagaw is the region most dependent on irrigation agriculture, Shibar is most dependent on other kinds of activities. The social implications of this contrast will be developed in the remainder of this chapter.

## SOCIAL CONSEQUENCES OF THE ECONOMIC ADAPTATIONS

The means of livelihood in different ecologic contexts constrain different social arrangements. Two economic factors affect the social alignments of Bamian's populations. The first is the degree of integration into a national market. In terms of this factor the Tagaw zone is distinct from the other zones, because of its dependence on cash crops and (at the markaz) marketing; the other zones depend almost entirely on subsistence crops. The dependence of Tagaw on cash agriculture and marketing economically links it (especially the markaz) to a larger, national network of commerce.

Although it is not the object of this study to describe this network, its broad features can be outlined to suggest its social relationship with Tagaw. The national network of commerce is primarily controlled by Sunni populations located in two economic and political centers, the Kabul-Koh Daman region to the east of Bamian and the Mazar-i-Sharif-Qunduz region to its north. Sunni power at these centers has supplied a protective cover for Sunni economic interests in Bamian. With the improvement of roads and other means of communication Bamian's Tagaw has become increasingly involved with these outside centers. Their Sunni faith, vis-a-vis the Imamism of their neighbors, evinces the degree of their social integration into the national economic system. Indeed, it will be argued later that Tagaw stands apart from the highlands precisely because it has historically belonged to a Sunni-dominated political system, while the highlands, rather than being integrated into it, have chosen socially to withdraw from it.

The people of Tagaw have not always been Sunnis or so well integrated into the national economy. Travelers' reports in the last century imply that the populations of Tagaw at that time were Imamis, though there seemed to have been a contingent of Sunnis in the markaz (Masson, 1842; Lal, 1834). How the Tagaw populations became Sunnis or, alternatively, how they supplanted the previous Imami populations, is not known. But that they are Sunnis today, unlike the rest of the basin, is at least consistent with their distinctly close ties to an enlarging Sunni economic network.

The other significant economic factor imposing on social arrangements in Bamian is irrigation agriculture. Irrigation agriculture, practiced by peasants throughout Bamian, draws those sharing common irrigation runnels into solidary groups.[2] Irrigation agriculture constrains groups to be solidary because of the properties of water.[3] A transient fluid substance, water on the surface of the earth, if used for agriculture, must be drawn out of its natural source and transported to the desired location before its release on the cultivated soil. Surface water is therefore usable only by artificial means. The necessity to control the flow of water artificially over a period of time requires those using it to be organized.

> Since the supply is . . . transient, and since it *flows past* and therefore may be beyond recovery, its use . . . automatically imposes problems of sharing (Bennett, 1969*a*:63, *underlining* original).

The persons using the water must agree on a plan and supervise its execution over time. Irrigation agriculture is therefore a social undertaking, molding the people sharing a water line into a community of interrelated persons.

[2] Cf. Adams (1962), Beardsley (1964), Geertz (1963), Gray (1963). This statement does not necessarily imply any point of view on Wittfogel's hypothisis that the emergence of state power is in relation to the development of large scale irrigation works. See Adams (1966), Steward (1955), Wittfogel (1957), Wolf and Palerm (1955).

[3] This discussion of the social consequences of surface water use has profited from Bennett (1969*a*).

Only the group sharing a common water line is rendered solidary by irrigation practice. Communities using different irrigation runnels tend to be distinctly separate from each other. This is most dramatically exemplified in the distribution of religious sects in Shibar. The religious factions in Labmushak (Fig. 3), for example, are generally distributed along separate irrigation lines: the runnels on the west side of the valley supply mostly Imami communities, and those on the east, Ismaili communities. The exceptions illustrate the point. The community of Juraqol, unlike the others on the west side, is Ismaili. Juraqol lands, however, are actually separately watered by a small natural stream, so it is independent of the Imami irrigation runnels. It is thus relatively free (for whatever reasons) to be different from the Imamis dwelling on the same side of the valley. However, Digu, which is also separately watered, is Imami; as its water supply is smaller than Juraqol's, its lands at critical times must be watered from the left bank canal system dominated by Imamis.

Internally fractured communities appear in Shibar and nowhere else in eastern Afghanistan because the rainfall agriculture of Shibar provides more latitude for community division. Rainfall agriculture, unlike irrigation, imposes few organizational demands, allowing people to work independently, and consequently to be socially less solidary. Dry-land cultivation can be done by individual farmers, for the land is watered naturally. Each owner can plow and work his rain-watered land without the cooperation or supervision of his neighbors, though certain tasks, e.g., in the use of draft animals for plowing, may require the cooperation of several farmers. The social requirements of rainfall agriculture, then, contrast with those of irrigation agriculture. Rainfall agriculture is an individual or small group enterprise without much regard for community interest, while irrigation farming is a social enterprise with less regard for individual interests.[4] It is in Shibar, where rainfall agriculture is vitally important, that fractured communities are found. Whatever the specific causes of division may be, the communities of Shibar have more latitude for internal fission because they are less strongly constrained to be solidary by the practice of irrigation activity.

A second factor affects the solidarity imposed by irrigation: the abundance of water in a shared irrigation runnel. Where water is abundant and easily accessible to everyone, a community need not cooperate closely to enforce codes of sharing, and may thus be relatively less solidary. Where water is scarce, the community must carefully supervise its water use and therefore is constrained to be more solidary. The divided communities of Labmushak (Fig. 4), for example,

[4]The cultivation of sarad lands and the care of flocks have social requirements similar to those of rainfall agriculture because they may be carried on with little regard for the opinions or demands of neighbors. But the sarad lands of Kalu are not vital for subsistence as they seldom can be planted with grain crops, and the flock care practiced throughout the highlands does not distinguish Shibar from the rest of the basin.

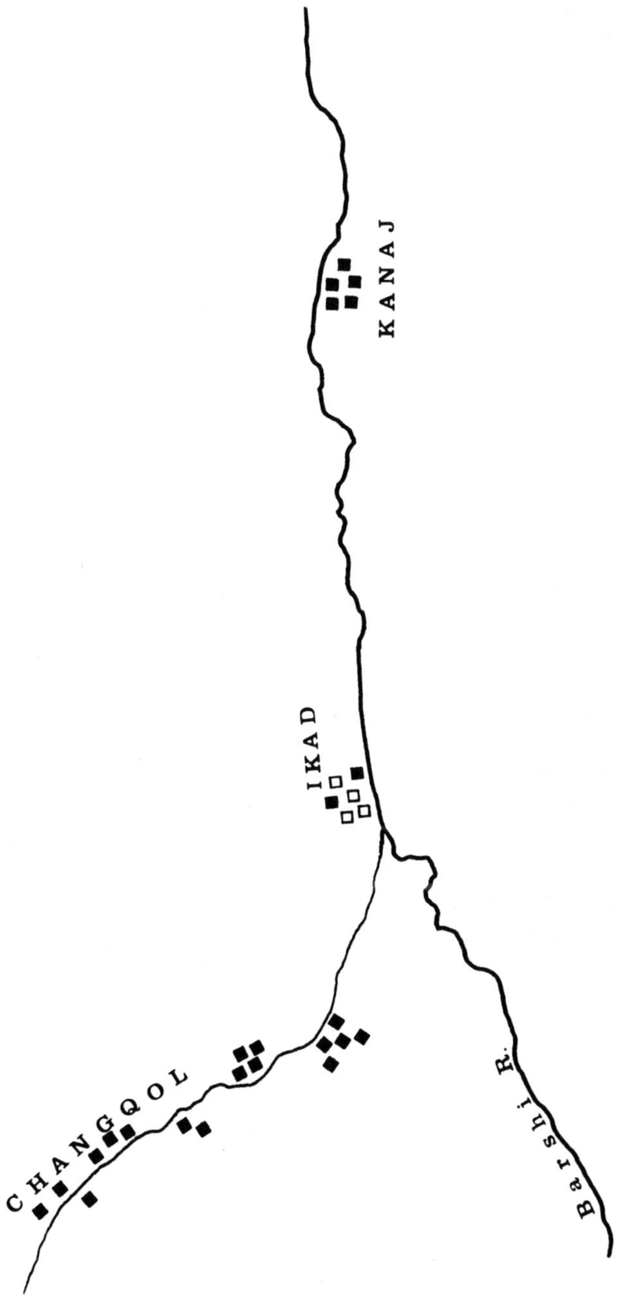


Figure 4. Changqol, Ikad and Kanaj.
Ismaili households are shaded; Imami households unshaded.

are situated along the naturally abundant waters of the Labmushak River. Dissident members of these communities have been able to tap directly off the stream without the consent of their neighbors. The communities on the plateaus above the alluvial plain, however, could not divide in this way because, supplied by lengthy canals carrying only limited amounts of water, they must more closely supervise the use of their water. Thus, where surface water is abundant and easily accessible to the community there is more latitude for community division than where surface water is scarce and the natural source distant.

Communities located near the natural water source are not always more free to divide. In the narrow valley of Changqol (Fig. 4), for example, all the farmers in the valley dwell close to the natural stream. But the stream is small. At critical periods in the summer, the water has to be shared by turns day and night. There is no social fractionation of communities in Changqol as a result; all inhabitants are Ismaili. Just below Changqol, however, at the village of Ikad, division has occurred. Ikad is watered by two natural streams, the Changqol rivulet, which at critical times is almost dry, most of it being used in Changqol, and the Barshi stream which is larger. After flowing through a narrow gorge where irrigation is not feasible, the Barshi stream disgorges on the plain of Ikad, and in combination with the Changqol stream, provides ample surface water for Ikad's needs. Social division within Ikad could take place because its water supply is abundant and easily accessible to individuals who are unwilling to cooperate with the community. Further down at Kanaj, however, the Barshi stream, having been used freely on the lands of Ikad, is small. The necessity to cooperate in its use has acted to hold the community of Kanaj together.

A qualification, therefore, must be appended to the argument. Communities in Shibar indeed are more free to break, due to their vital dependence on rainfall agriculture. But even in Shibar not all the communities divide, because the relative scarcity of water in the irrigation lines on which they partially subsist may still constrain them to hold together. In addition to being vitally dependent on rainfall as well as irrigated lands, those communities that have divided internally are located near natural flowing streams carrying an abundance of surface water.

# III

# SOCIAL SYSTEM I: TERRITORIAL GROUPS

THE conclusion was drawn in the previous chapter that the extent of a group's dependence on irrigation agriculture and the abundance of water in its canal seem to define the ecologic constraints which to varying degrees tend either to hold the group together or allow it to divide. This point merely suggests the ecologic circumstances in which communities may cohere or, as in Shibar, divide. Obviously, it leaves some questions unanswered. For example, it does not explain why any community would be inclined to fly apart. That the economic activities of flock care and rainfall agriculture are highly important in Shibar does not explain why these activities should eventuate in the breaking of fellowship between community members, even to the point of their aligning themselves in hostile sectarian factions and disavowing any meaningful ties of kinship. Moreover, it does not explain why neighborhoods should be checkered by contrasting religious alliances. And it does not explain specifically how the social ties joining persons in communities and neighborhoods actually may become ruptured so that the former bonds are dissolved and new social alignments are constructed.

The problem to be dealt with in the next three chapters is the internal circumstances of social division. These chapters focus on the social structure of neighborhoods and communities in Bamian and on the kinds of behavior which can lead to religious division among kinsmen. The analysis is presented in two schematic descriptions which apply to social relations in Bamian generally, the first a scheme of group arrangements and the second a scheme of dispute tactics, including conversion.

The analytical model of structural arrangements is the subject of this and the next chapter. The central aim of the description is to make a point already suggested by Wolf:

> Social relations create order, but sometimes in the very act of creating orderliness they breed disorder (1966:97; see also Holloway, 1968).

The description of local social structure tries to show that inherent in the social ties drawing persons together are tensions working to rend them apart. United or divided villages and neighborhoods are presented as variant forms of a general social system in which contrary tensions are operative. The system takes different forms—as divided neighborhoods and communities in one area, as united neighborhoods and communities in another—in response to the environmental factors which are conducive to one or the other pattern.

The social system is presented in four descriptive parts, the first two of which appear in this chapter. The first part describes the ideal conceptions of unity among kinsmen; the second, the structures of territorially based social groups; the third part, constituting Chapter IV, the structure of the kinship network, a non-territorial sharing group; and the fourth, Chapter V, the processes of fission and conversion.

## THE CONCEPT OF KINSHIP SOLIDARITY

The common local term for a spatially and socially united group of people is the term for the agnatic group, *qawm.*[1] The central intent of the word "qawm" is that the members are united by agnatic kinship, have a common home territory, and enjoy warm social fellowship. A qawm in its conception is a socially solidary group. The members of a qawm, in local usage, are qawmi to each other. Qawmi are in-group persons; non-qawmi are in some sense out-group persons. Qawmi should dwell in the same territory. They should cooperate in work when needed; they should be politically united, operating as wholes for political purposes; and they should be religiously united, celebrating the Muslim holidays together and gathering at appointed times to pray and listen to sermons or the reading of religious literature. The local members of a qawm, therefore, are ideally a territorially and socially integrated group, joined together through ties of kinship, political action, and religious belief and ritual.

A qawm, depending on the reckoning, may be as large as an entire ethnic group or as small as a hamlet group composed of only a half-dozen households. As a result, the functional unit which qawm groups really achieve varies according to size of the unit, smaller groups approximating the ideal better than larger ones.

Actually, the word "qawm," rather than describing an empirical social pattern, is a term for a locally conceived structural category (Levi-Strauss, 1963:271). It therefore may be adjusted to suit various actual social situations. It may be invoked, when appropriate, for various ranges and degrees of kinship reality, and denied when not appropriate. The word qawm may be used to include, not only those persons reckoning themselves agnates through a common ancestor, but also

[1] From the Arabic, *Qaum* "tribe, nation." The Arabs normally employ the word only in association with the name of a tribal chief, as "the *qaum* of Shalan," rather than with the name of the tribe (Musil, 1928:50).

the persons who mutually assist each other and share goods with each other, not all of whom are always close kinsmen. It may apply to affinal as well as agnatic kinsmen, and even to unrelated persons who become assimilated into a group by marriage. And it may refer to friendly families who may eventually form kinship ties through reciprocal marriages. Conversely, the word can be contracted so as to exclude certain actual kinsmen who no longer cooperate with the rest of one's in-group. The kind of adjustment the concept of qawm undergoes in deference to actual social practice was implied in a conversation overheard in Kabul among several persons who had emigrated from their provincial districts. One person said that he now had hardly any contact with his qawmi. Instead, his neighbors now meant more to him than his qawmi back home. Another in the group replied, "Well, these are your qawmi now. In Kabul your qawmi are your neighbors." In practice, the word "qawm" is applied to a group, whoever they are, who functionally carry on the activities that express kinship unity, even if this usage masks certain aberrancies in the actual kinship connections.

The activities which demonstrate the unity of kinsmen, however, do not necessarily express their personal feelings toward each other. Ideally, of course, qawmi should be sentimentally close as well as economically, politically, and religiously aligned. But personal sentiments among qawmi, despite their overt expressions of solidarity through the reciprocal sharing of goods and cooperation, can sometimes be bitter and hostile. Persons may only be participating in the qawm group by compulsion, despite personal dislikes for some of their neighbors and kinsmen, since cooperation with the others is a necessary expedient. Hostilities may be expressed by making insinuations in gossip, by refusing to participate in certain social functions, and the like, but so long as these qawmi cooperate in certain crucial instances they remain members of the qawm group. As one person expressed it, even brothers may fall out of fellowship with each other; they may even separate their residences or cease to communicate socially; but they still keep up the appearances of their brotherhood.

This chapter and the next discuss the units of social interaction and the behavioral forms which maintain the ideal of social unity, even if enmities do exist.

## TERRITORIAL UNITS OF SOCIAL INTERACTION

This section presents the territorial units of social interaction in a typologic series of inclusiveness, from elementary to compound units. Since they correspond with the general pattern of social interaction, they are generally reflected in the spatial groupings of persons. Consequently, to keep the levels clear, the social units are described as territorial as well as social units of interpersonal relationship.

Four levels of territorial grouping and interaction are distinguishable: nuclear families, households, qawm communities, and neighborhoods.

## The Nuclear Family

A nuclear family is composed of a man, his wife (or wives), and their children. Sometimes, one of the spouses having died, there may be only one living parent in the family. The head of the family is the man, but if he dies his wife (the older, if more than one) becomes head until a son reaches adulthood. Commonly, the man personally owns and works the land on which his family subsists. Some men are landless and have to hire out as laborers or as tenants to wealthier persons. For a number of days each summer–from 20 to 60, depending on need and accessibility of wild vegetation–the men must also gather thorn bushes used for heating and cooking. The women of the family cook, sew, and in summer do much of the weeding of the farmland. In the highlands where flocks are kept, the women milk the animals morning and evening. Children are required to help in the shepherding of the flocks at an early age; but when they become strong enough, usually when they reach puberty, sons begin to work on the soil with their fathers.

Several nuclear families often live together in a single house; however, for several months of summer in the highlands, each family lives separately in its own yurt (*chapri-chapari*).[2] In their aylaqs situated high in the mountains, where in summer they pasture their flocks, the yurts of close relatives are pitched together in small groups. After harvest, when it is cooler, the families pitch their yurts on the irrigated tracts of land near their houses and live in them for several more weeks in order to avoid the fleas, bed bugs, and other vermin that flourish in their houses during the hot season.

Each nuclear family in a household has at least one box in which personal effects are kept. These are locked, as they contain the few valuables belonging to the family. Personal belongings are not shared unless sentiments are close. Often the contents of these boxes are not revealed to other families in the house. Private gifts I made to individuals were sometimes secretly hidden from other members of the household. Similarly, the doors of individual families sharing a house are often kept locked when no one is there. If the families cook and eat separately, they have separate storage bins for flour, or separate bins in the walls of the house known as *bukharis.*

Although many families appear to be relatively tranquil, tensions surrounding the conjugal relationship sometimes disrupt the family. If serious, the

[2] The term "yurt" used here refers to a temporary, transportable summer dwelling. However, the temporary dwelling used in Bamian, though having affinities with the Central Asian yurt, is merely a crude approximation to it. Further north, temporary dwellings more closely approximate the true Central Asian yurt (see Ferdinand, 1959).

tensions may influence relations outside the family and thus breed hostility between persons in larger social groups. It is therefore necessary to explain the husband-wife relationship and the kinds of potentially disruptive tensions implied in it.

Men typically believe the women to be violent or fierce (*shalita*). There may be some justification for this feeling because the women have limited emotional outlets in their social relations and sometimes have no one but their husbands to whom they may release their feelings. Besides being deemed fierce, women are said to be untrustworthy. Sometimes, as the women manage the goods used in cooking, they may (especially if hostile to their husbands) hoard small amounts of flour or sugar, etc., in order to gain a few negotiable goods of their own. These they may use in exchange for other desirable goods or for favors. A woman might, for instance, pay some extra wheat to induce another woman briefly to care for a baby, or spin or sew for her, or make clothes or handkerchiefs. But if the husband or father should discover that she is using food for this purpose, his fear that the women in the house are untrustworthy is substantiated.

The feeling of distrust men have toward their wives is further aroused by occasional incidents of adultery. I heard numerous accounts of adultery, of which the following is an example:

> A. K. seduced the wife of M. K. and the husband happened to come in and see them, so there was a fight. They were fighting in the house while their infant child was sleeping there and the child got underfoot and was killed. A. K. was jailed for that for several years. Now the husband is in Turkestan. But after A. K. got out of prison, he came to Kabul and brought the woman and her children . . .

The fact that several families live close together also contributes to extramarital sexual relations. Husbands therefore tend to be watchful of their wives. Though they dominate the home and the marriage relationship, they are sometimes unsure of their wives' loyalty. Visitors sometimes (they say) run across lusty women where they are guests. A person whose work involves moving around to the different communities of the area enumerated several instances when, as he slept in someone's house, he was approached secretly by a woman of the household. How frequently such incidents really occur is impossible to estimate, but stories of sexual incontinence abound among the men, for example:

> Sheykh Barsisa was a holy man who prayed a lot and therefore was considered a perfectly reliable person. A man going on the pilgrimage wanted to leave his sister, who was very beautiful, with someone trustworthy while he was away, so he decided that there could be no place safer for her than the house of Sheykh Barsisa. But while she was staying in the house, Sheykh

> Barsisa noticed her, loved her, and finally took her by force. She became pregnant so he killed and buried her. When her brother finally returned from the pilgrimage the Sheykh told him she had died of a disease. . . .

It is believed that adultery is more frequent in the mountains than on the plains. If true, this may relate to the kind of subsistence activities there, in which more opportunities exist for women to be isolated from their husbands. As the women take the flocks and children into the mountains during the summers and the husbands are often gone into the mountains to gather brush for fuel during spring and summer, there are many long periods when spouses are separated.

In vernacular usage no distinction is made between rape and adultery. It is assumed that the woman has consented to the act whatever her personal inclinations may have been. When rape occurs it is a great insult and shame to the woman, of course, for it exposes her weakness and vulnerability as well as that of her family.[3] It is assumed that, had her family been strong, the attack would not have been possible or successful. The greatest shame is to the woman's closest male relatives, her husband, or, if not married, her father or brother. Her attacker, on the other hand, is proud of his conquest, for it demonstrates his strength and courage. If he were to be caught, he likely would be killed or badly abused by her family; for if they were not able to retaliate, it would be a monstrous humiliation. It does indeed happen that the insulted males, due to insufficient economic and social leverage, cannot avenge such an affront.

A woman who has been raped is said to be more acquiescent to subsequent demands of the same man again lest his disclosure of her conquest spoil her life and reputation. No one wants a woman who has been raped. If it becomes publicly known that she has been raped, other men will also go after her. She is known as *radi* (or *razi*), "tracked." More seriously, she is looked upon essentially as an adultress. And she has no legal recourse without the utmost public embarrassment.

Persons who maintain an illicit sexual relationship are known as *rafiqs*, "friends." The rafiq relationship naturally has numerous complications. A person may have a rafiq for a while but she may be married off to someone living far away, or she may be divorced and have to move, rendering the relationship more difficult. Of course rafiqs can never be seen together.

Because of the suspicion over illicit sexual activity, the women are typically circumspect in their social demeanor around men. Considering how closely people are able to watch each other, living close together in small groups, it seems strange that any mischief of this kind happens at all, yet a number of adultery (or

[3]The relation between a woman's purity and her agnate's honor appears to be comparable to that described by Campbell (1964). See also Peristiany (1966).

rape) cases are carried to the courts; many more never reach public view. This no doubt is why men tend to be extremely sensitive about their women and why most women are generally careful to remain aloof from any man who is not a close relative.

Tensions in the household caused by suspicions of unchastity between spouses affect relations between agnates. Males of a household or a community may unobtrusively withdraw from each other or openly come into conflict over a suspected illicit relationship with a woman. Abdul Ahad, for example, a poor young man, was married to a beautiful young woman who caught the attention of Imam Ali, a wealthy neighbor and kinsman who also was married and had a child. Eventually Imam Ali seduced Abdul Ahad's wife. When the affair became known, Abdul Ahad was obliged to divorce his wife, but he was powerless to gain retribution against Imam Ali because of the latter's much greater wealth and influence. Imam Ali married the woman, but because of the hostility of his entire community he had to rent out his land and move to Kabul. After a few years, however, he was able to return to his village. Abdul Ahad, humiliated by the incident, moved out of the village and remarried elsewhere.

Wives are sometimes beaten by their husbands. The practice of wife beating, judged by the number of persons who testified to it, may be fairly common. A wealthy *hajji* (pilgrim) explained, for example, that he has two wives, one whom he does not like, secured for him by his father, and another whom he does like, obtained by himself. The wives do not really like each other but out of fear of him, he said, they don't fight. Each of them has a separate room and separate dishes. He said that when they offend him, he beats them with a stick—a big one, he explained, gesticulating to show its great size. He hits them on the shoulders, head, and arms. Sometimes they don't get up from bed for several days. And they might not speak to him for a long time, or they might complain to him because he "beat them without a cause" (his words). But whenever he frowns, he said, they jump.

A young man once explained that a few days previously he had fought with his wife. He showed bruises on his legs where she had hit him with a stick. In response he had grabbed her by the hair and hit her with his fists. When she got away from him she ran to her father's house nearby. He was in the process of making occasional visits to his father-in-law's house to attempt to heal the breach between them. Another reason for going was that a few days after the fight she had given birth to a son.

Women have few means of recourse, if abused. If they should run away, they could be beaten or divorced. The husband in the latter case need only go to the court with a few witnesses. If a woman should complain to her father, she is not likely to get redress. A father, to avoid having to return the bride price for her, seldom attempts to save his daughter from a cruel husband. In the past a woman could not hope to obtain release from an unhappy marriage by complaining to the government, though this is less true now than formerly. Nowadays, sometimes a woman will deliberately wound herself to show the court that her husband is cruel.

Though separation or divorce is seldom possible for a woman, the tension over the abuse of a wife may bring the families of the spouses into conflict and eventually break the cord of solidarity which the marital bond was meant to strengthen. But the hostility between the families of feuding spouses is often publicly expressed over some other issue. Since vengeance for abuses of the conjugal bond relationship cannot be satisfactorily won, it must be gained under other pretexts. Thus, families related through an unsatisfactory or stormy marriage align themselves on opposite sides in other disputes. The tensions of marriage, therefore, may underlie other kinds of social conflict.

## The Joint Household

Houses are occupied by one or more nuclear families who may have some agnatic connection, usually a close one. The house (*khana*) in which nuclear families live is generally a two-story structure, the ground floor being for the animals and storage, and the upstairs for the human residents. Downstairs there is a "cow room" (*gawkhana*) where animals are kept at night during spring and fall, and continuously during winter. Also downstairs is a "forage room" (*alaf khana*) where winter food for the animals is stored. Upstairs on the second story there are quarters for the families inhabiting the house. These consist of a sleeping room, and a kitchen (*kar khana* "work room"). There may be separate storage space as well. Outside the houses large piles of dung cakes along with the bushes used for winter fuel are stacked in piles against the side of the house.

Where two or three nuclear families live in the same house, each may occupy a separate suite of rooms consisting (always) of a kitchen and (often) an additional room for storage or for entertaining guests. A widow and her children will inhabit a separate suite, but a widower's family usually eats, and sometimes lives, with an agnate's family. Poor families, however, commonly possess only one room, a kitchen. Sometimes, depending on the sentiments of the women, two or more families may share a single kitchen while occupying separate sleeping rooms.

The kitchen is usually the center of nuclear family activity, but sometimes, owing to lack of space and a meager supply of fuel in winter, several poor nuclear families will share a common kitchen. A kitchen is distinguishable from other rooms by the oven built into the floor. The oven's warmth serves to heat both the downstairs and the kitchen upstairs during the severe winters. Other appurtenances in the kitchen depend on the wealth of the household and the relationships between the nuclear families sharing the kitchen and the dwelling. It is not uncommon for poor families to use the kitchen as a sleeping-living room as welll as a room for preparing food, especially in winter when fuel is in short supply. In wealthier homes there is a separate guest room for entertaining visitors, but in the usual household one of the living-sleeping rooms of a nuclear family has to be used for entertaining guests.

Today a different style of house is being built which clearly aims at privacy. This is a two-storied construction with the rooms surrounding an interior courtyard where cooking can be carried on in the open air, but within the privacy of the house. These have been built by the wealthy families and seem to be the trend; several such structures were under construction in 1968.

The nuclear families who share a house are related through agnates. A young man and his family will usually live in the same house with his father and mother; in such cases his wife works in the same kitchen with his mother. Often brothers' families dwell in the same building. Or the families of agnatically related first or second cousins, or a man and his paternal nephew, may share a house (Fig. 5).

In winter the nuclear families in a single household may live together in one kitchen to conserve fuel. In the richer households, however, a room known as a *tawa khana* is used as a sitting room. This consists of an elevated room under which the heat from a fire is conducted before being exhumed outside. Though often quite comfortable in winter they are expensive to heat, and I found no family using a tawa khana on a regular basis. For most families, then, the use of fuel for heating the common kitchen entails the sharing of resources with another family. The sharing of fuel between several nuclear families requires that the men in these families cooperate in collecting the fuel from the mountains.

Members of the household or other close relatives, if of the same generation or younger than the speaker, are often addressed by *laqabs.* Laqabs are titles or nicknames used in addressing, and sometimes in referring to, a relative. A laqab is properly a title such as a king might bestow. It is also a title for an adult who has achieved some eminence, such as *malem sayb* (for a teacher), or *wakil sayb* (for a parliamentary representative) or *godaamdaar* (for the keeper of the government storehouse). A laqab is also used within the family, commonly bestowed by the women, as a term of endearment, chosen to suit one's character. It might be an affectionate name, such as *aaghaa shirin,* "sweet sir," or a descriptive term for some feature of a person's personality or appearance, as for example, *baatur,* "the wild." These laqabs are used among close relatives rather freely, depending on their sentimental relations. Generally, if they are on good terms the laqab is employed; if not, the personal name is used. Sometimes laqabs are used for certain unpopular characters of the community behind their backs or, teasingly, to their face, such as *paay-kata,* "big foot." A girl does not usually get a permanent laqab until after marriage. It is given her by her husband's mother; if she likes her new daughter, she will give her a laqab early; if not, she will continue to call her only by name. If a husband and wife are on good terms they will call each

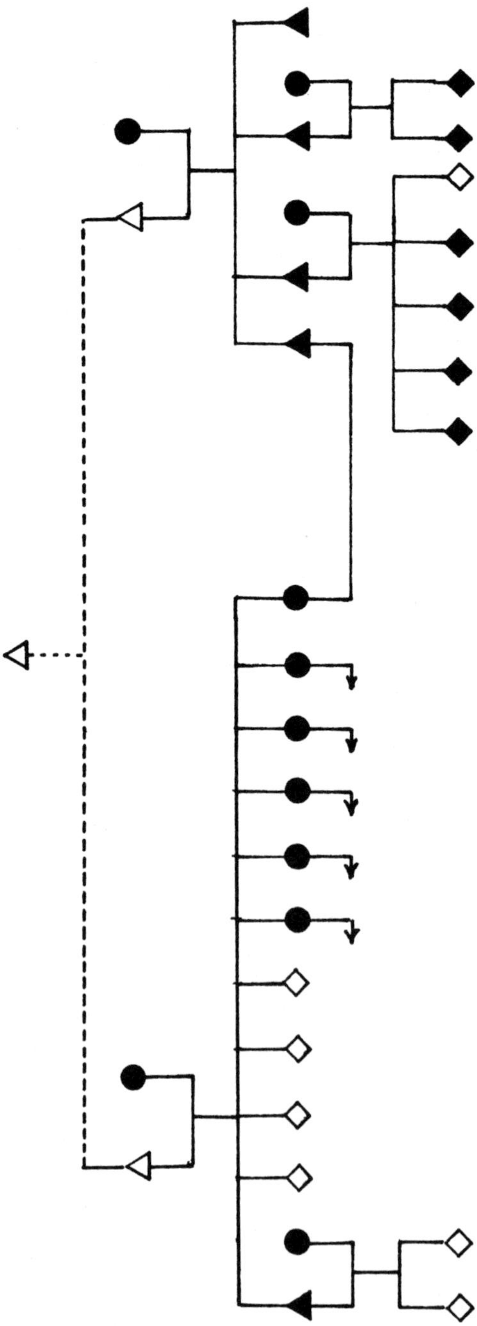

Figure 5. Relationships of the inhabitants of a house in Rezaka.
Deceased persons are unshaded. Arrows indicate persons who have married out.

other by their laqabs or, honorifically, by teknonymic terms, "Mother of ___," or "Father of ___." Parents will call a daughter by name until she bears a child, and then by her teknonym.

Generally the men and women of the families in a household work and socialize in separate groups by sex. The men of a household, being agnatically related, usually own adjacent lands, and generally have not divided the property inherited from a father or grandfather. They work cooperatively, irrigating the land together or by turns, collecting by turns the wild thorn bushes used for fuel, working together in construction and repair of the house, plowing and harvesting their crops together, and the like.

The women of a household often work together in the same kitchen, the oldest being in charge. To make the weeding of the fields more pleasant, they work together on each other's fields. They also weave rugs (*gelam* type) together, the number of women available, usually three to five, determining the width of the rug; sitting side by side in a row they all work on a single weft at the same time. They likewise assist each other during sickness. These families also retain a similar pattern of cooperation in their summer highland pastures (aylaqs) and occupy adjacent yurts. The sheep and goats of the families in a household are always pastured together, but the animals of each family are separately milked by the women twice each day.

Older persons of a household are treated with deference. Even after sons reach maturity and establish families of their own they will show public respect for their parents. As long as the father is able to work he usually directs the agricultural activities of his family. Among the women age is important, but the woman who controls the preparation and distribution of food is usually the dominant woman of the household.

> In my family [said one man] my mother used to be the strongest of the women because she was the cook. Now my first wife is the strongest because my mother is quite old and my wife is cook now. My mother has to be nice to her so that my wife will feed her well. Of course I get the best food, because she would be out if I weren't happy, but the rest of it she shares with my mother. This food is one way that she gets power over her.

Tensions among the women of a household continuously develop over the work routine. A mother, for instance, may be disappointed in the way a new daughter-in-law does the household chores. She may miss her own daughter who has married out and find the new daughter-in-law a poor replacement. A daughter, having learned to do the chores from her mother, is familiar with the household routine, but a daughter-in-law may be slow to learn and even reluctant to follow some of the work patterns familiar to the household.

Tensions between the women can contribute to the fissioning of relatives. A wealthy man told me that a woman usually wants to get her husband to move out of a joint household so that she won't have to share the work and the utensils with the other women. To divide brothers sharing a household, a woman may fight with the brother's wife or even the brother himself. Or she may attempt to prejudice the brother's relationship by hinting to her husband that the brother or his wife is taking more than his share of something. A family moving out in such circumstances, if it builds a new structure, may move only a small distance away and thereby eventually be able to resume cordial relationships with the original household. If a family cannot remove itself to a separate structure, it might divide the house by walling off separate quarters for each of the families, and opening a separate door to the outside. This practice, however, is not common.

If tensions between the women become severe enough, the males of the household are likely also to become involved. Typically, however, even though brothers may not speak to each other, they will, as mentioned earlier, continue to carry on certain kinds of cooperative activities. Often there is an eventual rapprochement.

Still, bitterness between close relatives does sometimes persist for life. A woman told me that her father's relatives, even when they visited their house on social occasions, tended to quarrel with them. They seldom felt, she said, that they had a trustworthy friend among their own relatives. Her mother had been so angry at her father's relatives that before her death, she requested that she be buried in a strange graveyard rather than with his kinsmen.

## The Qawm Community

Spatially grouped agnates retaining close ties of social interaction and social identity are here called a "qawm community." A qawm community is the smallest group calling themselves a qawm.

*Settlements.* Most qawm communities dwell in hamlets[4] but some live in village fortresses (*qalaas*). Village fortresses are large dwellings, spacious enough to house as many as 30 families, equipped with high, fortified walls, and wells in the interior courtyard. They were built to withstand the former slave-raiding assaults of Uzbek and Turkoman marauders from the north.

Village fortresses were constructed by order of the Mir, or chief, of the district, who was strong enough to oblige and pay his weaker neighbors and kinsmen to work his land as well as build such a structure. They appear to reflect the more stratified social structure formerly extant among the inhabitants of the region (Aslanov, et al., 1969; Ferdinand, 1959; Schurmann, 1962). Few village

[4] *Deh,* "village," is not here distinguished from *geshlaq* or *agel,* here translated "hamlet," because the only difference in local usage is relative size. Apparently, further west *agel* means "a small, domed-shaped branch hut" (Ferdinand, 1959:28).

fortresses exist in Bamian anymore, because, with the termination of slave raiding, they were gradually abandoned in favor of less compact settlements. Eventually they were dismembered for parts useful in constructing new buildings. Remains of village fortresses are seldom even visible, but the sites of former fortresses are sometimes indicated by such place names as Qalaay-Mullah and Qalaay-Maamad.

*Kinship composition.* The male members of a qawm community putatively are all agnates. Figure 6 shows the ties between the adult members of a small qawm community which occupies two hamlets known as Lower and Upper Ali Jam. The native-born members of this community, descendants from a common ancestor, Ali Jam, call themselves the qawm of Ali Jam. They are socially united by ties of common descent, marriage and cooperation, but territorially they are separated in two hamlets.

While descent through a male line from a common ancestor is usually claimed, not all the members of qawm community are necessarily so related. Interlopers sometimes are assimilated into qawm communities through marriage. Their descendants are then considered agnatic descendants from the eponymous ancestor of the community. A single individual, for example, may be accepted as a laborer in the qawm community and eventually, if favorably received, marry into a sonless family. His sons would then receive his father-in-law's property as if, in effect, no interruption in the male line had occurred. It was explained to me in a specific case as follows:

> Shah Abdul is not from Pesh Zyar himself. He is really from Day Mir Daad, so his qawm is different from the rest. His grandfather came here. It is possible he became at odds with his qawm and took a wife here in Pesh Zyar and stayed here. Shah Abdul is now a Pesh Zyari himself, though he was not originally from here.

This tendency for a qawm community to incorporate strangers into the existing group is facilitated by the practice of first-cousin marriage. If an outsider is allowed to marry into the group, his offspring can (and should, by ideal standards) intermarry with his new affinal kinsmen. It thus becomes easy to form close agnatic relationships within a single generation and so to accept the interloper as an actual link in the chain of descent. He is grafted into the agnatic line by simply reckoning him the son of his wife's father.[5]

*Kinship terminology.* The terms of relationship within the qawm community witness to their sense of relationship through agnates. Qawmi commonly

[5] Bacon (1958) was the first to note this as a general pattern among the Hazaras.

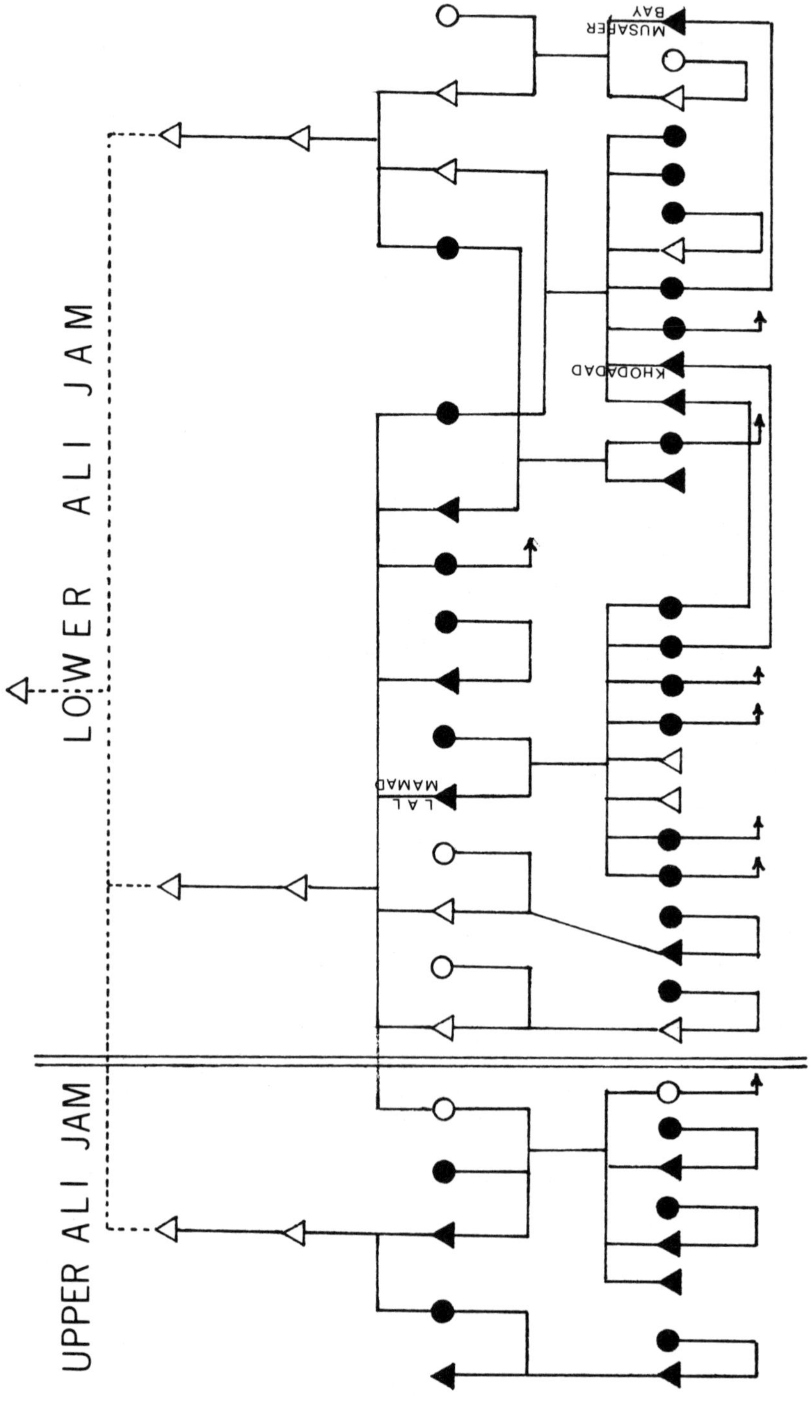


Figure 6. Kinship relations of members of Ali Jam qawm (children excluded). Deceased persons are unshaded. Persons who married out are indicated by arrows.

address one another with the terms of reference indicated on Table 2, but with the following provisions.[6]

1. Qawmi older than ego are addressed by a kinship term; those younger, by name.
2. Persons actually related to ego lineally or those collaterally through only one collateral link (e.g., FaBr, FaSi, MoBr, MoSi) are addressed by the kinship term designating this relationship, e.g., *tagha* (for MoBr), *khaala* (MoSi), *awdur* (FaBr), *amma* (FaSi), etc.
3. Everyone else in the qawm community, except those persons two ascending generations from ego, is addressed, if older, by one of the terms for first ascending generation collaterals on father's side. That is, generally, all qawmi males older than ego are addressed as *awdur (=abagha=kaakaa)* (FaBr), all native-born qawmi females as *amma* (FaSi), and all wives of awdurs as *enga* (or *sanow*) (FaBrWi). All persons younger are addressed by name.
4. Qawmi persons two ascending generations from ego are addressed, if males, as *baaba,* or, if females, as *aaja.*

In this usage, generally everyone in one's qawm community, except his closest relatives, is addressed as his grandparent or grandchild (if two generations removed), as his father's brother, father's sister, brother's son, or brother's daughter (if one generation removed), or as a patrilateral first cousin. Virtually everyone in a qawm community, except females who have married in, is reckoned as a kinsman on his father's side.

*Intermarriage.* First cousin marriage, that is, to a child of one's terminological awdur (FaBr), is considered the ideal. According to Islamic proscriptions a man is not allowed to marry his mother, sister, sister's daughter, brother's daughter, mother's sister, brother's sister, father's sister, or a former wet nurse and any of her similar relatives. Marriage to cousins of any degree is therefore permissible, and marriage between close relatives is in fact common (see Table 3) in order to avoid dispersing land rights to outsiders, and so to maintain the corporate identity of the local descent group.[7] One person, upon learning that first cousin

[6]These are the terms in use in a specific community in Shibar. Actually, although there is much variation in terms used in different areas, the distinctions of the system are retained throughout Bamian.

[7]Islamic inheritance law defines in elaborate detail the order of rights and the amounts to be received from an inheritance. The stipulations that a certain amount of the inheritance should go to relatives of a certain degree gives the relatives a specific set of rights to one another's private properties. Intermarriage within this group effectively insures that these rights shall be compounded within the group by a reduplication of their kinship ties through marriage.

TABLE 2

KINSHIP TERMS OF REFERENCE

**Lineal Terms**

*aata* = Fa; *aaya* = Mo; *baaba* = MoFa, FaFa; *aaja* = FaMo, MoMo; *baaba kata* = FaFaFa, MoFaFa, FaMoFa, MoMoFa; *aaja kata* = FaFaMo, MoMoMo, FaMoMo, MoFaMo; *bacha* = So; *dokhtar* = Da; *nowsa* = SoCh, DaCh; kowsa = SoChCh, DaChCh

**Sibling Terms**

*kaaka* = ElBr; *aapa* = ElZs; *braar* = YoBr; *khwaar* = YoSi

**Collateral Terms**

*awdur* (or *abagha* or *kaakaa*) = FaBr; *awdurzaada* (or *awdurbaacha* or *bachey-kaakaa*) = FaBrSo; *amma* = FaSi; FaSiDa; *khwaarzaada* = SiCh, FaSiCh
*tagha* (or *maamaa*) = MoBr, MoMoBr, MoFaBrSo, MoBrFaBrSo; *bachey-tagha* = MoBrSo; *dokhtar-e-tagha* = MoBrDa; *khaala* = MoSi, MoFaBrDa, MoBrWi; *bowla* = MoSiCh; *bachey-khaala* = MoSiSo; *dokhtar-e-khaala* = MoSiDo

**Affinal Terms**

*shuy* = Hu; *zan* (or *khaanom*) = Wi;
*khosor* = WiFa, HuFa; *khosorbara* = WiBr, HuBr; *khosor kata* = WiFaBr, HuFaBr; *khosor maada* (or *khoshdaaman*) = WiMo, HuMo; *khosor maada kata* = WiFaSi; *dokhtar-e-khosor* = HuSi; *eywar* = HuBr; *eygachi* = WiSi, WiFaSi;
*daamaat* = DaHu, SiHu, BrDaHu, SoDaHu; *beyri* (or *sanow*) = SoWi, BrWi, BrSoWi; *ezna* = husbands of female collaterals; *enga* = wives of male collaterals

marriage was not practiced in our culture, expressed the belief that this was why we had no qawm communities in our country. Examples of the frequency of marriages within a qawm community are provided in Table 3. In one community 44 percent of the marriages were between qawmi, and in the other 33 percent.

As a consequence of the frequent intermarriage between cousins, kinship ties within the qawm community are typically intricate, for its members are related to each other by multiple ties of descent and affinity. The diagram of kinship relations in Ali Jam qawm community (Fig. 6) illustrates the amount of intermarriage and the resulting multiple kinship ties within a small agnatic group. The children of Khodadad are related to Musafer Bay through two lines, an agnatic line through their great grandfather, in which case Musafer Bay is their awdur (FaBr), and a cognatic line through their father's sister, in which case he is their ezna. They address Musafer Bay as awdur. Their relationship to Laal

TABLE 3

EXAMPLES OF MARRIAGE FREQUENCIES WITHIN AND OUTSIDE QAWM COMMUNITIES

| Name of Qawm Community | | Total Marriages | Between Qawmi | Qawmi Girls Married Out | Non-Qawmi Girls Married In |
|---|---|---|---|---|---|
| Maya | (no.) | 43 | 19 | 9 | 15 |
| | (%) | (100) | (44) | (21) | (35) |
| Reza | (no.) | 43 | 14 | 9 | 20 |
| | (%) | (100) | (33) | (21) | (46) |

Mamad, however, is terminologically the same; through whichever parent they reckon kinship, either their father (a sister's son of Laal Mamad) or their mother (his daughter), he is their *tagha.*

The close and intricate relationships between members of a qawm community are further intertwined by the practice of exchanging girls between two families, known as *ostoghan alish kardan,* "exchanging bones." The girls are exchanged in marriage to avoid the bride price costs to both families. This kind of exchange, when between families in the same qawm community, naturally compounds their relationship ties. A specific case of this kind of sister exchange was given in the following statement:

> I went to live with my *awdur* (FaBr) after my father died. I took [in marriage] his daughter as my wife, and my sister married the son of my *awdur*. . . . It was my right to marry her; no one else had such a claim on her as I did. . . . We took wives from each other and paid no money for the girls except the expenses of the marriage. We had grown up together, so we all knew each other. At the time of the marriage we gathered the people, killed several sheep at one time and had one feast. We gave the food to everyone. We cooked maybe 150 pounds of rice. They ate the food and prayed for us, and they joined us in the two marriages.

Members of the qawm community traditionally claim first rights to the girls of the community. Ideally, first cousins have first priority to marry a girl, and after them, the other males of the qawm community before any non-qawmi suitors. This was expressed in the quote above, in which the speaker said, "no one else had such a claim on her (his FaBrDa) as I did."

The traditional order of rights to a girl, however, has recently been breaking down and it is invoked or denied according to its use to the suitor. The same person who in the quote above claimed a prior right to a FaBrDa denied the importance of this rule when he attempted to marry another more distantly related girl.

> There was another man who was attempting to get her. He was in her qawm . . . her parents wouldn't agree to him, so he went to the Hakim [a sub-governor] with a petition to have the police come and get me [for attempting to marry her without her qawmi's consent], but a friend of mine stopped him on the way. He gave him some money and took the petition away from him. . . . He would have complained that the parents would not give him their daughter. Actually, he didn't have this right. They could give her to anyone they wanted to. He was just a useless man. . . . He had the idea that if they wouldn't give her to him, then they shouldn't give her to anyone else.

If a man dies, his brother, and then his other qawmi have prior right to marry his widow. This rule, once perhaps followed strictly, seems not firmly practiced now, with the result that numerous disputes over such widow rights occur. A dispute, for example, arose between Maya qawm community and Lablabu qawm community over a Lablabu girl whose husband from Maya qawm died. After his death she came home to Lablabu. She was still young, and in Lablabu several suitors asked for her, so eventually she was engaged to one of them. The brother of the first husband, who of course belonged to Maya qawm community, tried to break up the engagement by claiming he had a prior right to her. But the Lablabu qawm community insisted on keeping her, under the excuse that her father had already promised her and this could not be changed. They agreed that if he had claimed her earlier, he could have had her. A group of elders from Maya qawm came to Lablabu to make their claim on her and take her away, but after a great argument they agreed to accept a payment of cash from her qawm instead.

*Property transfer.* The lands of qawmi, especially irrigated lands, tend to be spatially clustered, probably because they have been divided from the property of the male ancestor of the qawm community, and because current practices of land transfer tend to favor the continuation of this clustering. Upon the death of a property owner, if there are sons, daughters will not usually receive any portion of it, though according to the Hanafi interpretation of Islamic law a daughter is entitled to half the inheritance of a son. And recently, as governmental regulations have been more widely enforced, more women have been claiming this property right. Should there be no sons, of course, the inheritance falls to the daughters of the deceased. Women who have no brothers, and consequently receive their father's inheritance, sometimes remain in their father's house, and their husbands move in with them.

The clustering of agnates' lands is further accomplished by an official requirement that, should a man have to sell some of his land (only a rare and extreme resort in case of a financial exigency), the first opportunity of purchase must be extended to the owners of adjacent plots. So the property of a seller often falls to a neighbor, often a close agnate.

Certain kinds of land transfer, however, tend to disrupt this pattern. The land may not be purchased by a neighbor, or it may be turned over to an outsider as security for a loan (an arrangement called *geraw*) and, owing to financial exigencies of the original owner, never be redeemed. In such cases the land falls to an outsider, but this occurs relatively infrequently.

*Irrigation activities.* Although agricultural land is privately owned and worked, the members of a qawm community have a corporate interest, as described earlier, in the canals that water their adjacent plots. It was argued earlier that as the waterways have to be constructed and maintained by cooperative labor and shared under group supervision, the people whose lands are watered by a common canal are socially bonded together. Actually, persons who own land served by a single canal must work together on its repair. If someone refuses to participate in this work, one of their members can complain to the elders of the community or, failing that measure, to the government. Cleaning a canal and shoring up its embankment is done by the group in the spring, as needed. Generally canals on the lowland plain require relatively little attention, but those on the hillsides sometimes require quite a lot because the winter snows and spring rains tend to erode the embankments and clutter the canals with silt and debris.

Individually owned irrigated plots run linearly in double or triple parallel rows on the lower side of the main canal from which they are watered. Minor arteries are kept open for the feeding of plots from the larger canal. This spatial arrangement, and often the limited amount of water carried by the canal, obliges farmers to water their plots by turns from the common source.

The length of canals is often correlated with the number of people brought into association through irrigation from the one canal. The lands adjacent to the river itself obviously can be supplied by shorter canals than those farther away, and can be dug more easily by the owners of such plots. But the farther a tract of irrigable land lies from the natural source, the longer the canal feeding it has to be to reach it; consequently a larger number of persons must cooperate in its construction and maintenance.

This system of water sharing sometimes presses men into conflict. The adjacent plots of qawmi drawing water from the same canal are delimited solely by one- or two-foot dikes surrounding the plots on all sides. Since as yet there is no cadastral survey indicating the exact boundaries of plots, the owners must be careful to ensure that these dikes never shift. But in the attempt to gain maximum tillable space the farmers, when plowing, tend to crowd the dikes, pushing them, albeit slightly, onto neighboring plots. As a result, plowing season is fraught with disputes over land boundaries.

The routine encounters necessitated in the sharing of resources and labor, though sometimes expressing feelings of accord and fellowship among friends, often intensify the hostile sentiments of enemies. Tension between some qawmi seems to be perpetual. Men, for example, who have disputed over the use of water or the boundaries of plots will likely have to argue again, for the same problems of turns and rights to scarce resources have to be faced routinely. The hostility between qawmi is expressed in some sayings. People sometimes say, *Doshman dareyn? Ma awdurzada darum,* "Do you have an enemy? I have a cousin." They may also say sarcastically, *maa shir-i-khoda baladastem,* "We are familiar with the milk of our cow," meaning "We know the people who are close to us; no one has to tell us about them."

Even brothers are sometimes forced into competitive positions over scarce land and water. This is not so true in moderately wealthy families where brothers inherit large enough portions to provide each with a comfortable living. But where families are poor and land is already minimal, the tension between brothers over land can be serious. In such instances brothers, despite the belief that they should help each other and get along together, may become bitterly hostile.

In sum, the members of qawm communities who must cooperate in the use of a common water source are brought into tension with each other over the embankments which delimit their adjacent properties. Hostility and tension exist over the boundaries of a scarce resource–land–among the very group of people who are obliged to hold together for the joint employment of another scarce resource–water. The term *pulwaan shariki* (or in Hazaragi, *jagha shariki*), "embankment sharing," meaning the practice of cooperation between neighbors, implies a contradiction between how people feel toward each other and how they must act toward each other. That is, they may happen to distrust and dislike each other and yet be obliged to cooperate in their own separate interests.

*Other cooperative activities.* Within the qawm community several families, usually closely related ones, besides participating in the water-sharing activities of the community, also cooperate in other routine subsistence activities. The occasions in the year when a farmer needs a hand from his neighbors are numerous. The fall of the year is a critical time for a highland farmer: his crop is usually ready for harvest only a few days before the initial frost of winter; he must also thresh and sift his wheat before the cold sets in. So during harvest time in the higher localities where frost may be imminent, farmers find it useful to arrange to work each other's plots together in order of their urgency.

The differences in the growing seasons of the lands in the highlands is one factor that enables highlanders to assist each other profitably during harvest season for these lands mature in turn up the valley. Were there no seasonal variability of plots on the highlands this kind of cooperation would be less feasible; everyone's harvest would come in at once, and so everyone would be working on his own harvest at the same time. As it is, crops on rainfall lands or on high spring-watered lands mature at a different time than crops on the irrigated plots. Furthermore, as barley matures earlier than wheat, and unshaded lands earlier than shaded lands, the local farmers have some latitude for working out the sequence of their cooperative efforts, so that they assist one another reciprocally at the appropriate time when each plot must be harvested. On Tagaw, of course, the crops mature at about the same time, but because the frost comes later, Tagaw farmers have more time to harvest them.

Besides the urgency of harvesting and threshing before winter frost in the highlands, another reason mutual help is useful is that threshing is best done by several households together. One man, it is true, can thresh his wheat with a single bull by means of a device known as a *shaatul,* a platform made of a thorny bush on which someone rides to give it weight as it is pulled around the threshing floor. But this is not as efficient as using a team of five or six bulls driven as a group side by side around the threshing floor. Farmers who have small crops will therefore pool their bulls and, where possible, borrow more for a few days from farmers whose threshing is either completed or not quite ready; and together they will thresh their crops in turn (but keeping each separate) on a single threshing floor. Wealthier men who have plenty of land and enough cattle will also need additional labor help for threshing, but such farmers usually get help by paying a poorer farmer as a day laborer or by requesting favors of weaker relatives who can eventually be repaid in other ways.

The sharing of pack or draft animals among a few families, especially the poorer ones, is also a necessity at certain times in the year. As few families have more than one bull, they have to share their animals reciprocally for plowing. Moreover, as a man can take two or three donkeys up onto the mountain to gather thorn bushes or forage as efficiently as he can take only one, an owner of one donkey is inclined to arrange with another owner of one or two donkeys to use all their animals together by turns, each taking them on alternate days to do his own work. This sharing of animals, whether bulls or donkeys, is known as doing *polghu.* It is also common for a few households to graze their sheep together. The families inhabiting a house always keep their sheep in the same flock, it being unfeasible to separate them during the day because they are stabled together at night. But beyond this there is some latitude in flock-grazing arrangements. Sometimes all the families of a qawm community will hire a single shepherd and combine their sheep in one flock; sometimes smaller groups of families will have joint flocks. In a few cases families of different but nearby qawm communities will cooperate in this way. Similarly, small herds of bulls and donkeys, known as *paadagaws,* are made up of the animals of the families of one or two qawm communities. This is a form of cooperation characteristic only of the highlands, as few sheep and goats are kept on the lowlands of Tagaw.

Shepherds of the smaller flocks are commonly children under 15, usually from one of the households contributing animals to the flock. In such cases, the child or his parent is paid in grain by the other families after harvest. For the larger flocks an older person is hired as shepherd. Usually the hired shepherds come from the qawm community; those who do not, in addition to their pay, are fed and bedded each night in turns by the different families owning sheep in the flock.

During spring and fall the sheep and goats are grazed during the day and brought back to their owners' houses at night; during summer when they are taken higher into the mountain aylaqs, they are kept on the small tracts of open ground around which the yurts of the cooperating families are grouped. These groups of yurts vary with the size of the groups cooperating in the common flock. Typically the common flock agreements and the spatial clustering of the yurts of the cooperating families reflect the current factional alignments of persons in the neighborhood.

*Special friendships.* Within the qawm community enduring and close friendships often form between a few individuals. A special dyadic tie between close friends is known as a *khaanda,* "step" or "adopted," friendship. A *khwaar khaanda* is an adopted sister, a *braadar khaanda* an adopted brother. Khwaar khaandas or braadar khaandas address each other as "sister" or "brother" respectively, confide in each other, work together when possible, share their goods with each other, etc. This is not a formal relationship, but is noticed by other members of the community.

Khwaar khaandas seem generally more intimate than braadar khaandas. A woman may have more than one khwaar khaanda, but usually no more than three or four. Khwaar khaandas may borrow and loan among each other, and they will share their goods without strict accounting. They invite each other over for special occasions and they are supposed to keep each other's secrets. But they often tell their husbands and sometimes other friends what they hear from each other, so their husbands and other relatives learn a lot about what is going on in each others' houses, e.g., about their troubles, their debts, what their children say, what happened over there last Friday, etc.

Besides being able to confide in each other, khwaar khaandas can help each other by "leaking" useful information to the right persons without revealing the source. A woman might say to an acquaintance in the interest of her khwaar khaanda, for example, "I hear that so-and-so is interested in your daughter. Do you know him? I don't really know him well, but he seems like a nice boy."

Women sit and work together and talk during the day, but when it is time to eat, the hostess always provides the food. A visitor would never take food from her house to the hostess' house. But a woman who has visited in her khwaar khaanda's house and wants to return the favor, might at another time take her a special gift of food. When a cow gives birth to a calf, for example, she might take over some of the beestings, which is considered especially tasteful when mixed with regular milk. Her khwaar khaanda in return might send her some regular milk from her own cow so that both could enjoy the mixture. Naturally, in close friendships there is less strict reckoning of obligations to share equally than that which is formally required among kinsmen.

Khwaar khaandas, if especially close over a long period of time, may swear to be sisters forever on the Quran but this is not commonly practiced. The children of khwaar khaandas will call the other woman *khaala* (MoSi) and her husband *kaakaa* or awdur (FaBr) unless he has a more honorific title, such as *aaji sayb* "pilgrim sir." The husbands of khwaar khaandas are not necessarily friendly, and in fact may resent their wives' intimacy. The following is a description of a particular khwaar khaanda relationship:

> My mother had a khwaar khaanda and she would stay with her at night and we had to invite her husband and children over to our house too. She was from the same village, the wife of the mullah. Whatever happened in our house, we heard it at the other end of the village, and we knew that our mother had told no one except her khwaar khaanda. The khwaar khaanda lived only a few minutes' walk away, but we would go over there and stay one or two nights. And they would come and stay with us. Often my father would come home for the night. But we would stay over there late and talk.
>
> The reason my mother was so close to her khwaar khaanda was that all of the other persons in the village were my father's relatives; she could not be close to any of her husband's relatives because she did not want his people to know how she felt. When she finally discovered a woman who could be her khwaar khaanda it was natural that this would be a non-relative of my father. In this case, as the village was split in two factions, her khwaar khaanda had married into the other group. A woman who is in her husband's village doesn't have much chance to have her relatives over, so my mother didn't have anyone to tell her feelings to. So she needed a person to talk to who wouldn't let it get back to my father and his people. But often it did anyway.

Braadar khaandas similarly have intimate relationships. They invite each other over to their homes too, but as the men often work independently they cannot see each other so frequently. I was told that sometimes the wives of braadar khaandas become friends too. When they find a girl for their sons or marry out their daughters they often use their braadar khaandas as go-between to the parents of the prospective spouse. And of course they often arrange for their children to intermarry, thus binding the affective ties of the khaanda friendship more formally through affinity.

Of course braadar khaandas confide in each other. An example of a specific braadar khaanda relationship is the following:

> Aziz became braadar khaanda to Abdul Akim about ten years ago. They had been classmates through the sixth grade. When Aziz went away to study in Kabul, they made a promise to be braadar khaandas for ever. When Aziz came to Kabul, Abdul Akim, who had started to work in the local government office, gave him some money. Now that Aziz has finished his education and has a better government job he feels he should help Abdul Akim. Aziz loans him money without interest, entertains him, visits him on his days off, etc. They tell each other things they would not tell anyone else—a father, a brother, or awdur in their qawm, for example. They talk about girls, some of the plans they have for the future, and so on.

Not everyone has a braadar khaanda or khwaar khaanda, but the few khaanda relationships in each qawm community, by leaking information not otherwise communicable between estranged persons, provide a mechanism for releasing the tensions of internecine hostility and gossip sometimes present in the qawm community.

*Common prayer.* The males of the qawm community regularly gather for public prayers. The five daily ritual prayers enjoined upon the muslim are formally expressed in prescribed physical prostrations and recitations which visibly display one's faith. More spiritual merit is promised for the prayers of groups than for the sum of individual prayers recited privately. Friday is the day for the muslim to pray publicly with his brethren. Each village has a mosque which is a room or building for Friday prayers. Usually the room is only large enough to hold about 50 people sitting on the floor. When on special occasions larger groups gather for religious meetings, they meet outdoors.

The mosque is repaired and serviced by communal labor. In the month of Mizan (beginning about August 21), soon after harvest the leading elders call for all men of the community to bring fuel bushes, one donkey-load per family. Then cleaning and mudding of the mosque is done to bring it into respectable condition in case of a visit by a government inspector.

The weekly prayers of the adult males are done somewhat differently according to the sect. As the overt motions of the prayers of each sect are different, they identify the members of each sect, and express the religious solidarity of all its members. Sunnis say group prayers and hear a sermon at the mosque by the leader of prayers on Fridays just after noon. Imami groups meet in the mosque on Thursday evenings ("Friday nights") and Friday mornings, to listen to the reading of stories, to cry over the sufferings of Hosayn and other venerated martyrs of the sect, and finally to pray.

Imami group prayers differ from those of Sunnis, *inter alia,* in the importance that is placed on the personal qualities of the leader of prayers, the *mullah imaam.* The mullah imaam must be an unusually pious ("pure") person as he is considered the substitute for the Imaam, who is believed sinless. Before the prayers each person privately repeats the statement, "I have accepted the present *imaam*," i.e., the man standing as leader of prayers for the group. The spiritual efficacy of the group prayers is thereby placed on the shoulders of the mullah imaam. He must recite the entire prayer sequence while those behind him recite only part of it, and he must not let his full attention wander from the recitation of prayer during the ritual, lest his and the prayers of those praying with him be rendered ineffectual.

Ismailis from two or three adjacent hamlets or villages, if near enough, gather in a mosque or a home on Thursday evenings for prayers and the reading of books. In the prayers I observed, no one took a position in front of the rest, though one person led the group recitations. After prayers the men read, besides the Quran, portions of books written by the Ismaili Saint, and some other poets. Literate persons in the group take turns reading to the rest, and there is some discussion. "These meetings are for prayer and learning, not for solving disputes," someone said. Sometimes their meetings last until early morning.

Another kind of prayer, *duwaa* (Arabic *du'aa*), is a brief, perfunctory prayer, but it is considered efficacious in avoiding misfortune. The giving of feasts is considered a means of gaining good fortune through the prayers (duwaas) of thanksgiving expressed by the guests. People sponsor feasts partly to repay social obligations but more importantly, they say, to elicit the guests' sincere duwaas for God's blessing on the host and his household. Aside from the supposed supernatural effect of such prayers, they have the social effect of reassuring the members of the group of the intercessor's goodwill and their willingness to conform to the mores of social fellowship.

*Elders.* The heads of the several households in a qawm community comprise the elders of the community. As there are variations in wealth, there is variation in the amount of deference given different older persons, but usually, whether rich or poor, they are respected. Persons of influence in the community are generally of a mature age. The elders form an informal body that makes decisions on community-wide affairs. Social gatherings provide them opportunities to develop common understandings and opinions on issues of current interest, so generally everyone in the community knows everyone else's opinions. Commonly, on Fridays after the prayers the elders go to someone's house to drink tea and talk; sometimes they simply linger after prayers at the mosque.

The elders sometimes meet for special purposes. If they as a group become embroiled in a dispute with another group, requiring political action, they will meet to discuss policy and strategy. If the government conscripts a certain number of men from the qawm community to work on a construction project, such as a road or a government building, they will meet to decide who has to go.

For certain assessments made against all the members of the qawm community the leading elders take the responsibility of collecting the funds. For example, for the salary payment of the local mullah a list of the qawmi who can contribute is made and three or four respected elders, those most noted for honesty and fairness, will circulate among the qawmi, collecting and noting down the amounts contributed by each.

In discussion, the older and wealthier persons have the most influence. Usually only the older men talk, but among them there sometimes is one person whose opinion is often sought and, when given, accepted. A person of such influence is commonly one who controls much more wealth than the others.

In the qawm community one elder is a recognized representative of the group to the government. He is known as the *arbaab*. Communication between the government officials and the qawm community usually is transmitted through the arbaab. Arbaabs are involved in the collection of taxes and fees and the conscription of persons for military service or government labor. Above the arbaab is the *mir*, or *mallek*, who usually represents several qawm communities to the government. Arbaabs are usually contacted through the mirs by the government officials, and the arbaabs in return take information back to the mir rather than directly to the government officials. Recently, however, arbaabs have been dealing with government officials on their own.

## The Neighborhood

A neighborhood is a highland valley inhabited mainly by several qawm communities, most of whom are related. Neighborhoods are not really significant social units on Tagaw, as Tagaw is a relatively large unbroken plain; populations on the Tagaw are, however, spatially grouped into common descent groups, a social unit to be described in this section. Neighborhoods are analytically considered separate levels of social interaction in the highlands because neighborhood spatial groupings are dictated by the topographic segmentation of valleys in the highlands, and because the inhabitants of these valleys usually claim certain common pastures which loosely draw them into social association.

*Common descent groups.* As mentioned earlier, the size of a group of kinsmen who make up a qawm varies according to the range of kinship one wishes to refer to. One may call the members of his village his qawmi or all the persons in his valley his qawmi, or even the persons located in neighboring valleys his qawmi. Figure 7 illustrates the relationship of smaller and larger descent groups to each other within the valley of Labmushak.

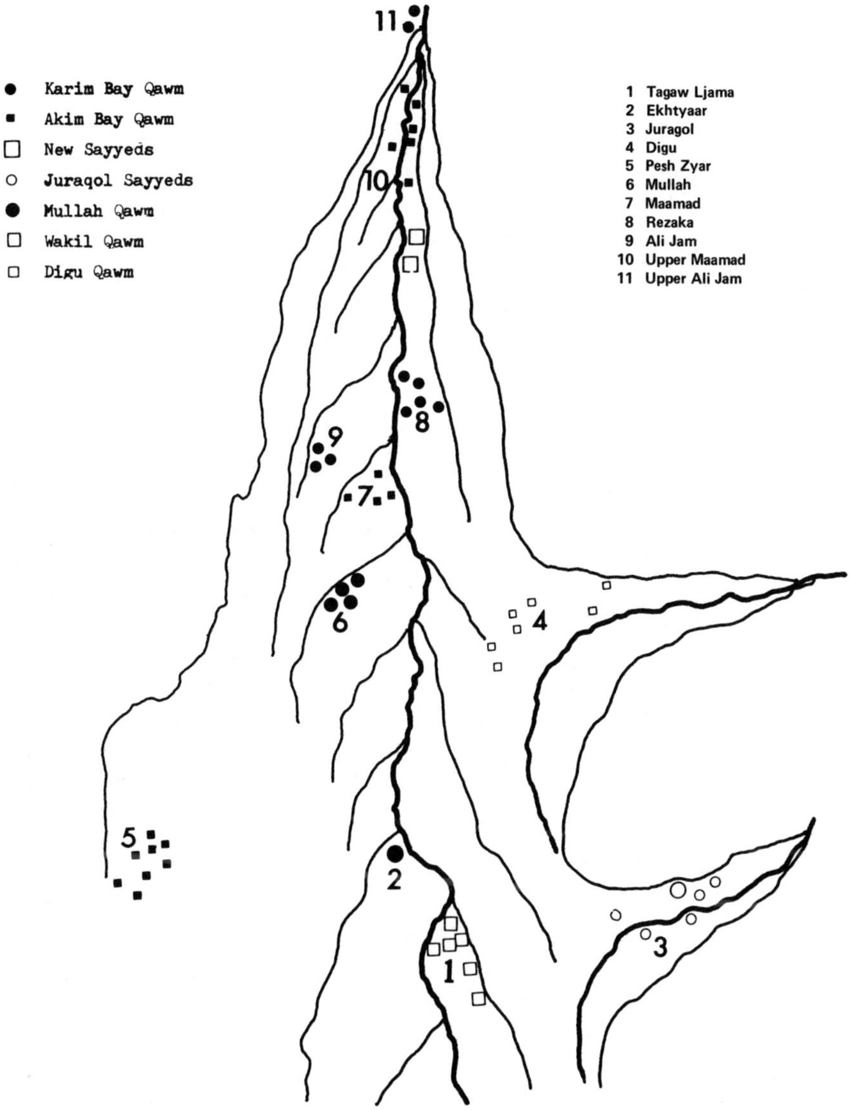


Figure 7. Descent groups in Labmushak.

The Hazara descent groups who claim to have come earliest to this valley were those of Akim Bay and Karim Bay, both descendants of Khida, the putative son of Baba Dargan (Darghu in Hazaragi) (see Fig. 8). So they, as well as the inhabitants of a number of adjacent valleys, are reckoned sons of Khida. Another group descended from Khida are those known as Sheykh Maamad who dwell in other valleys not far away. Few people are clear as to the specific lines of ancestry that link Akim Bay and Karim Bay to Khida. In fact, only a half-dozen elderly people (some women as well as men) could give a chain of ancestry all the way back to Khida. Most other people could remember five to seven generations of their forefathers, but the younger people typically could remember no further back than their own grandfathers. Some people were not sure whether Akim Bay and Karim Bay were brothers or whether Karim Bay was a son of Akim Bay. Even so, there is a general belief that in Labmushak there are two stems of descent emanating from Khida, those through Akim Bay and those through Karim Bay.

It appears that spatial location was one means by which the residents identified a person's membership in the different descent groups, for upon coming to uncertainties in someone's chain of ancestry they would say that the sons of Karim Bay simply are in the villages of Ali Jam, Rezaka, and Qalaay-Ekhtyaar while the sons of Akim Bay are in Pesh Zyar, Qalaay-Maamad and Qalaay-Mullah. The implication is that the members of these territorial units are descent groups representing sublines of descent from the eponymous ancestor.

The sons of Karim Bay may have once been mirs of the valley, since my informants recognize Ekhtyaar (an old word for elder or chief) as a descendant of Karim Bay. The old qalaa of Ekhtyaar is situated on the choice lowlands not far from the mouth of the valley, but the males claiming descent from him are only two, through a common grandfather. Their families occupy opposite corners of the now practically ruined fortified dwelling. The other sons of Karim Bay live much farther up the valley in Rezaka and Ali Jam. The hamlet of Rezaka is a cluster of about 10 houses. Ali Jam is broken into two hamlets, the original one now consisting of three structures not far from Rezaka and the newer one, Upper Ali Jam, situated on the highest irrigated tract in the valley.

Two of the several sons (or descendants) of Akim Bay, the other son of Khida, were Lutfali and Faizili, and their descendants occupy Pesh Zyar. The descendants of Maamad, another son of Akim Bay, are now scattered in the higher portions of the valley. The village called Qalaay-Maamad is the largest cluster of his descendants, but higher up the valley, between Lower Ali Jam and Upper Ali Jam is a string of houses grouped in twos and threes, most of which also claim descent from Maamad. Also among them are two houses of Sayyeds and a family descended from another offspring of Akim Bay, Baybaad, most of whose other descendants live in a small neighboring valley.

Mullah Baabay, the founder of Qalaay-Mullah, was sometimes given as a descendant of Akim Bay, but elderly informants indicated that this is not

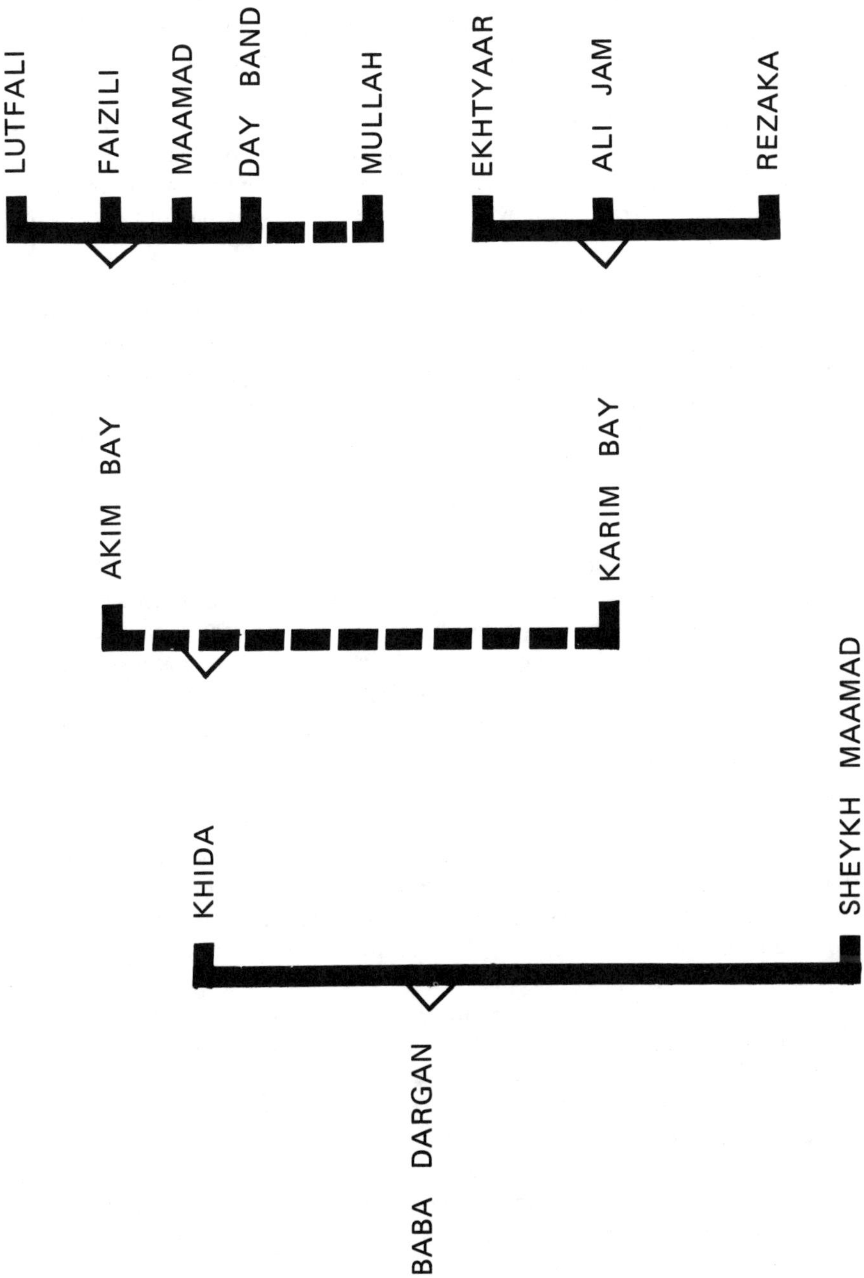


Figure 8. The descendants of Baba Dargan.

accurate. He was probably an outsider brought in to serve the religious interests of the community a long time ago. His descendants have continued to be leaders in religious practice and opinion (being able to read), though like almost everyone else, they are mainly farmers.

Digu descent group is similarly said by some to represent another line from Karim Bay but older persons indicate that Digu qawm is also from the outside. Some say Digu are from Lajoo valley over the mountain, but the most knowledgeable persons insisted that they are from the Qaaluq subgroup of the Sheykh Ali Hazaras.

The groups inhabiting the best lowland tracts of Labmushak are from the outside. The ancestry of the residents of Tagaw Khana has been forgotten but their ancestry is different from the other groups. The Sayyeds residing in Juraqol, and the two related households high in the valley, are also of vague ancestry. The solitary household of Sayyeds near Tagaw Khana has come into the valley only recently through land purchases and marriages with the wealthy families of Tagaw Khana.

These outside groups moved into the valley after the descendants of Khida had become ensconced there. The fact that they occupy favorable locations suggests that they immigrated from a position of strength and displaced other groups. Possibly they were stationed there by powerful outside Hazara groups, the notable ones nearby being the Sheykh Alis and the Besuds. A Sayyed family might have been invited to come in and settle in Juraqol, as is sometimes done, for its religious value to the neighborhood. Unlike individual interlopers grafted onto existing common descent groups, these groups have been able to raise children in their own names because they occupied territorial blocks which fell to their male heirs.

One more descent group is represented by the two Arab men serving the valley as blacksmiths, one in Pesh Zyar and the other in Katayalaw. Many of their forefathers have had Hazara wives, and physically they are indistinguishable from Hazaras. They have no land. Their specialized occupations, passed from father to son, seem to provide the basis for retaining their kinship distinctness.

In an earlier quotation on the ancestry of someone who had interloped into a qawm community (see p. 45) the speaker suggested that the interloper may have left his home territory because of conflict with his own kinsmen. This is a significant supposition, for it suggests a reason for the spatial fragmentation of certain descent groups, as in, for example, the divided descent groups of Ekhtyaar, Maamad, and Ali Jam in Labmushak. It is likely that the built-in potential for conflict over resources may have caused occasional relocation of some of the group members so as to avoid or reduce tension. This option no longer exists because it is now much less feasible to bring new lands into cultivation than formerly.

*Common holdings.* The wider network of affinals and descent groups occupying the highland valleys corporately claim territories in the mountains where thorn bushes, if available, may be gathered for fuel and their flocks grazed. It is in these areas above the valleys that the rain-watered lands of Shibar are located.

Above the irrigated plains of the highland valleys, the hillsides, ravines, and glens of the mountain are particularly resplendent with brush vegetation in summer. The inhabitants of each valley claim the right to collect the wild vegetation used for fuel in the whole upper region extending from the skirt of the mountains to the very top of the ridge. They resent any fuel gathering in the areas by outsiders from less favored regions. If they catch a thief of fuel bushes they may take his ropes, which are highly valued, or report him to the government.

Not everything growing on the mountains above a valley, however, belongs to the entire neighborhood. As already mentioned, rights to pasturage on the highest slopes of the mountain belong to the nomads migrating into the area in summer. Below this region the local farmers have pasturage and cultivation rights of their own. In this region, topography and climate permitting, they cultivate rainfall land in the flattish wadis and ravines that are likely to collect the most precipitation when it rains in summer and snows in winter. All the rain-watered land that can be plowed is already under cultivation. The rest is pasturage claimed by the residents of the valley. If someone were to plow up a new tract for agriculture, the residents of the valley would complain because they would lose the benefit of the pasturage.

In Shibar, the belt of neighborhood-controlled lands includes both pasturage, where the yurts are set up in summer, and rainfall land. The rainfall plots of each qawm community, though privately owned and cultivated, are commonly grouped together, presumably because the area was once owned by a common ancestor. Among these rainfall lands there often are small stretches of pasturage where the land owner's flocks are sometimes grazed.

In addition to the pasturage claimed by each qawm community there are extensive untillable stretches of ground among the lower mountain ravines and slopes which may be grazed by any flocks from the valley, but not by flocks from any other valley. It is in these pastures that the people of a valley leave their bulls and female donkeys for the summer. The communities highest on the plateaus are close enough to these vales and hillsides to shepherd their bulls and donkeys in herds (paadagaws) and bring them back to their homes at night. But the owners of livestock in a valley farther away from the highland pastures, owing to the great distance of the pasturage from their homes, often let their bulls roam free through these mountain regions; the animals are left untended for many weeks of the summer because it is too cold at night for a shepherd.

The right to gather animal forage from the mountains for winter is like the right to pasture one's animals. One can collect wild forage in some places, but not in others because of the specific rights of the qawm communities in certain areas. Cutting grass on the pasturage of another qawm community is considered thievery, but cutting forage from pastures not specifically claimed by any qawm community is not.

It should be clear that the bonds of social cohesion in neighborhoods are relatively fragile. Even though ideally united through common descent, the populations of neighborhoods are in fact functionally drawn together only through their common pastures. Thus, the neighborhood as a functional unit exists among the highland populations where pasturage is an important secondary means of subsistence. There are additional ties, however, which more firmly draw the populations of neighborhoods together, but they are ties of a different kind than those described above. These are the social ties wrought through the sharing of goods and services among members of the kinship network.

# IV

# SOCIAL SYSTEM II: THE KINSHIP NETWORK

THE term "kinship network" is used to refer to the connected system of interrelated kinsmen, however they may be joined, whether through agnatic descent or marriage. Following Barnes (1954; see also Mayer, 1966), a distinction is made between a "set" of kinship connections and a "network" of kinship connections. A set of kinship connections is the composite of agnatic and affinal ties linking a single family with its relatives. A family's set of kinship ties obviously is not identical to the kinship ties of any other family, though their sets of connections may largely overlap. A network of kinship connections is the combined sets of affinal and agnatic ties of a group of interconnected families. The kinship network of a qawm community, for example, is the combined sets of connections involving all the members of that group.

A family's set of kinsmen is known as its *qawm-o-khesh,* "agnates and affines." Sometimes its set of kinsmen is simply glossed as its qawm. Thus, in popular usage one's qawm group may include, depending on the intent, his affinal as well as his agnatic relatives. A qawm community's network of kinship connections, when the group's combined kinship ties are being referred to, may also be called the qawm-o-khesh of that group.

The kinship network has three distinguishing features: it has no specific geographical context; it is only operative through ephemeral public gatherings; and it is a network of economic distribution.

## SOCIAL COMPOSITION AND GEOGRAPHIC CONTEXT

Kinship networks have no specific geographical context; they encompass both the interlaced, dense connections of kinsmen in qawm communities and also the dispersed affinal connections extending between different qawm communities. The kinship network is therefore a different grouping of persons than the territorial units described earlier; it overlaps with some of the ties of persons in qawm communities and neighborhoods, but it also reaches farther out into other districts.

The dispersal of kinship ties of course is a result of the numerous marriages consummated between members of different qawm communities. Figure 9 shows the dispersal of affinal connections joining a qawm community, Rezaka, to a number of other similar communities. Out of 43 marriages of the members of Rezaka qawm community, 14 (33 percent) were consummated within the group, six of which were between the offspring of brothers; 20 girls from eight different qawm communities were married into the group; and nine girls from the community were married out to eight other qawm communities.

The intricacy of the kinship ties within a qawm community contributes to its sense of unity vis-a-vis other qawm communities. Consequently, the members of a qawm community may consider themselves affines of groups into which one of their members has married. Members of affinally related qawm communities address each other by affinal terms of kinship. Older persons, if not directly related to ego through marriage, are addressed as maternal uncle (*tagha, maamaa*) or as maternal aunt (*khaala*) or, if two ascendant generations removed, as spouse's father (*khosor*) or spouse's mother (*khosorbara*). Affinal connections between qawm communities, then, are considered to draw the groups together.

> If a man [said one informant] gives a woman to a man of another qawm community they try to keep good relations between the two qawm communities. They will visit each other at special times, especially at times of a death or a marriage. But the women go for other lesser occasions, also; so they tend to form closer ties among themselves. Once the visits start, the exchanges of goods begin, and they tend to continue. In this way the ties of fellowship between the groups are maintained.

The kinship network, though not associated with any particular features of space, functionally contributes to the unity of two territorial groups, the neighborhood and the qawm community. Primarily it reinforces the unity of the qawm community because the ties of affinity and descent within the qawm community are, as already stated, exceedingly intricate. They also draw non-qawmi persons, many of whom of course live in other qawm communities in the neighborhood, into relationship with the community, thus strengthening the ties between communities in the neighborhood. The frequency of intermarriage among qawm communities within and outside a neighborhood is shown in Table 4. Affinal ties within the neighborhood are more numerous than those outside. However, marital ties between distant qawm communities, when once established, are often reduplicated, so that marriages sometimes recur between distant qawm communities.

A point not evident on the table, however, is that the qawm communities of a neighborhood are not all equally well integrated into a single web of affinity. Antagonisms develop between qawm communities and channel their relationships into different sets of intermarrying groups. Marriages are usually

| A Man From This Group | Married a Woman From This Group | | | | | | | | | | | | |
|---|---|---|---|---|---|---|---|---|---|---|---|---|---|
| | Rezaka | Pesh Zyar | Madarqom | Katayalaw | Mullagala | Tagaw Khana | Namaqol | Khakak | Lawed Bolaq | Lichikbir | Ghorbandak | Sheykh Ali | Turughman |
| Rezaka | 14* | 4** | 3 | 0 | 0 | 0 | 1 | 1 | 2 | 4*** | 4*** | | 1 |
| Pesh Zyar | 2 | | | | | | | | | | | | |
| Madarqom | 0 | | | | | | | | | | | | |
| Katayalaw | 1 | | | | | | | | | | | | |
| Mullagala | 1 | | | | | | | | | | | | |
| Tagaw Khana | 1 | | | | | | | | | | | | |
| Namaqol | 1 | | | | | | | | | | | | |
| Khakak | 0 | | | | | | | | | | | | |
| Lawed Bolaq | 1 | | | | | | | | | | | | |
| Lichikbir | 0 | | | | | | | | | | | | |
| Ghorbandak | 1 | | | | | | | | | | | | |
| Sheykh Ali | 1 | | | | | | | | | | | | |
| Turughman | 0 | | | | | | | | | | | | |

cross cousin marriages

*Six of these were FaBrDa marriages.

**Two brothers married two sisters.

***Two of the four marriages were to MoBrDas of the other.

Figure 9. The affinal connections of the members of Rezaka qawm community.

TABLE 4

RELATIVE DISTANCE OF QAWM COMMUNITIES RELATED THROUGH MARRIAGE TO REZAKA QAWM COMMUNITY

| Marriages to qawm communities in the neighborhood | | Marriages to qawm communities in adjacent neighborhoods | | Marriages to qawm communities in near but not adjacent neighborhoods | | Marriages to qawm communities distant but within Shibar | | Marriages to qawm communities outside of Shibar | | Total |
|---|---|---|---|---|---|---|---|---|---|---|
| Pesh Zyar | 6 | Namaqol | 2 | Khakak | 1 | Lawed Bulaq | 3 | Sheykh Ali | 1 | |
| Madarqom | 3 | | | Lichikbir | 4 | Ghorbandak | 5 | Turughman | 1 | |
| Katayalaw | 1 | | | | | | | | | |
| Mullah Qalaa | 1 | | | | | | | | | |
| Tagaw Khana | 1 | | | | | | | | | |
| Total | 12 | | 2 | | 5 | | 8 | | 2 | 29 |
| Percent | 42 | | 7 | | 17 | | 27 | | 7 | 100 |

consummated between friendly families, seldom between antagonistic families. Thus a marriage is best conceived as the structural formalization of an existing friendship. Families on good terms tend to reinforce their goodwill by repeated marriages every generation or so. But, if they should fall out with each other, their previously formed marital ties may quickly be disregarded and eventually be forgotten. Similarly, unrelated families who become associated for other reasons eventually express their ties through intermarriage. For instance, in a conversation regarding two families who had recently become allies in a dispute, someone observed that the families were not related yet, but would eventually become so. Affinal connections, then, are basically plastic, responsive to the vicissitudes of inter-family sentimental relationships.

The effect of this fact on the network of affinal ties in a neighborhood is that marital connections between hostile qawm communities in a neighborhood do not develop, or, if once extant, are not reinforced by additional ties, while marital connections between persons belonging to friendly qawm communities are kept strong by recurrent marriages. Thus the qawm communities of a neighborhood are sometimes aligned in separate sets of intermarrying kinship networks.

A kinship network has diffuse connections across a wide geographical field, conceivably extending to any locality. The outer limits of the network are in fact not geographical but social: since persons of different sects do not usually intermarry, the real maximal limits of the network are essentially the boundaries of the sect. The kinship network blends closely into the sect, for the kinship network is indeed, to a major degree, a religious network. Almost all the public occasions in which kinsmen in the network are brought together are religious or quasi-religious. And it is through such occasions that the influence of the leaders of the sect, the Saints, is mainly exerted. When the kinsmen are gathered on public occasions, it is common for a religious authority, if no more than the local elder closest to the Saint, or for a learned teacher, a mullah representing the Saint, to be present, and to lead in prayer or perform other religious services within the community.

The kinship network, then, being in its widest sense coterminous with the sect, reaches to the outer limits of social cohesion and cultural identification. The elastic word "qawm," as a result, when denoting the group who are practicing kinsmen, i.e., those in the kinship network, becomes also coterminous with the word for sect (*mazhab*). In Bamian, and generally throughout Afghanistan, the unity of a common faith implies a common kinship. I was told by one person, "We believe our blood is Imami, and their blood is Sunni." In the valley of Foladi a Hazara informant consistently used the word "qawm" to distinguish between the religious sects. Tajiks and Afghans were Sunni qawms, he explained. The Imami qawm of Bamian, i.e., the Hazaras (and Sayyeds?) were from Kandahar. The Ismaili qawm of Shibar, he felt, was a different kind of Hazara from the Imami qawm; he knew not whence it had come. This man lived too far away from the eastern highlands to know that the populations there, besides including the Ismailis he identified as a different type of Hazara, contained many persons claiming the same faith as he and that most of the members of both groups (excluding the Arabs and Sayyeds) claim the same ancestry.

## BONDS OF ECONOMIC OBLIGATION

The members of the kinship network are united through obligations to help and share reciprocally. The ties of obligation ideally follow the lines of social relationship: as the connections of descent and affinity between household and qawm community members are intricate, so their obligations to each other are generalized. That is,

> The expectation of a direct material return [for a gift] is unseemly. The material side of the transaction is represented by the social: reckoning of debts outstanding cannot be overt and is typically left out of account . . . the expectation of reciprocity is indefinite (Sahlins, 1965*b*:147).

Between affines who are not otherwise agnatically related, obligations may be less generalized and more strictly reckoned than those between the agnates of a qawm community. Even so, between affines of different qawm communities obligations tend to be generalized, depending on the closeness of the relationship. What actually differentiates the obligations of agnates from those of affines is merely the difference in the intricacy of their relationship ties. As the ties are typically more interwoven among agnates, their obligations are more general and more binding. The circulation of goods and services between kinsmen expresses their sense of moral obligation to each other, more obligation closer in, less farther out. Solidarity and reciprocity go together (Sahlins, 1965*b*:139).

As noted earlier, kinship connections are more intricate among geographically close kinsmen than among those more distant. The stronger obligations of close kinsmen, therefore, generally coincide with spatial proximity. Spatially close kinsmen tend to be more solidary than distant kinsmen because they are more able to participate in the social activities of mutual sharing and helping which bind them together.

The kinship network is manifest in only ephemeral social gatherings. Affinal and agnatic kinsmen interact with each other in informal social encounters, in life crisis rites and religious rites, and in mutual assistance activities. The life crisis rites and religious rites are described separately in Appendix I. The other forms of social interaction are included in the following description of the mutual obligations of kinsmen. These are the obligations to visit each other, to share food and goods, and to give labor assistance when needed.

## The Obligation to Visit

The core social activity of all social interaction is the visit in which personal respects are paid and food is shared. Visiting is an essential means of displaying goodwill between friends and relatives. Persons who visit a kinsman are showing their goodwill. An offended person expresses disaffection by refusing to visit a kinsman's house when it is expected.

In general, except for special occasions such as a marriage or funeral, when everyone must come to a person's house, a younger person should visit an older, and a poorer should visit a richer. If it were otherwise, people might say the elder or stronger person was *goshna,* "hungry, greedy," i.e., he wants something. This, of course, does not apply to equals, friends, and siblings, who should visit each other reciprocally, for a visit implies the payment of a courtesy which should be repaid.

There are a number of occasions on which kinsmen are in contact. For practical reasons men have to move around rather often, perhaps to buy or borrow straw or grain from someone in another neighborhood, to buy or sell a cow or donkey, to borrow money or pay a debt, etc. These movements allow them to make brief courtesy calls on kinsmen or special friends, and when feasible, to stay for tea, lunch, or the night.

There are also times when a person should make a point of visiting his kinsmen. He should visit, for example, when a kinsman has returned safely from a trip. It used to be that when someone returned from Kabul, his relatives and neighbors would gather and throw pastry (*chalpak*) on him to congratulate him on his successful journey, so distant and forbidding was Kabul in those days. This is no longer done, though they do still drop in to greet a newcomer; the traveler, in return, should have a small present (*sawghaat*) such as an orange or a handful of nuts, to give to his friends. When a man comes back from the pilgrimage to Mecca or from his army service, or returns well from the hospital after a sickness, his neighbors and friends are expected to pay a visit; also, when he has purchased something valuable, such as a car, or built a new house or graduated from school. On religious holidays people are supposed to visit each other, customarily several houses in a single day. People should also attend the life-crisis commemorations of their kinsmen, e.g., the childhood rites (men attend only those of a boy), engagements, weddings, funerals, and other religious rites. Their attendance at such occasions expresses their loyalty to the host; a poorly-attended social occasion is a humiliation to a host.

When someone pays a visit he is always given something to eat. A visit may be brief and casual, involving only a few minutes of conversation or it may be an overnight stay, but it always includes a presentation of food by the host. A visitor should at least be given tea; at mealtime he should be given food. Failure to provide a visitor with food at mealtimes, no matter what the inconvenience or cost, is an insult to him and a shame to the host.

The common consumption of food by kinsmen is an expression of solidarity. People who eat together are supposed to be friends; one does not eat with an enemy. The solidarity implied in the mutual consumption of food is expressed in certain words derived from the word for salt, *namak.* A *namakkhoor*, "salt-eater," or a *hamnamak*, "also-together-salt," is a person who eats with you and thereby is in league with you, i.e., a friend. A *namak bahalaal,* "acceptable salt," is a person who stays on good terms with his hamnamak; *namak ba harum,* "forbidden salt," is a person who does not.

## The Obligation to Share

When kinsmen attend a social occasion the two sexes gather in separate parts of the house. The men sit in a guest room, sipping tea, and eventually eat together. The women gather in the kitchen, and help the hostess prepare the meal; they also exchange gifts and, after the men, eat together. Both groups gossip freely. There are therefore two distinct circles of fellowship when kinsmen meet. Each is a distinct circle of reciprocal sharing. Among the men food is shared through the sponsorship of feasts, and among the women petty cash or pastries are given as personal gifts. Both circles express solidarity by reciprocal presentations of goods, and both control reciprocity in the presentations through gossip (see below).

The feasts sponsored by the men ideally consist of rice, bread, meat, and tea. The most important ingredient is the meat. The size of a feast is cited in terms of the number of pounds of rice served and the number of animals killed (*kushtani*). Through feasts meat, a perishable good, is transformed into social obligation. There are virtually no means of preserving meat in Bamian. Except in the markaz, where meat is butchered and sold daily, dressed meat is only available when feasts are given, or when raw meat is distributed after the death of a relative on *Id-i-Qorban* (see Appendix I). Consequently, as in most societies lacking preservative techniques, meat sharing is a device by which meat, a perishable good, is transformed into a preservable commodity, obligation. Those who attend a man's feasts are expected to invite him to the feasts they sponsor; if they are too poor to sponsor feasts, they must give other favors as they can. As a young man expressed it to me, "The food given at a feast is a kind of loan, though no one really wants to express it that way."

In the parallel circle of prestations among the women—which is scarcely known among the men—the items given as gifts vary according to the kind of petty goods accessible to them. The Tajik women in the markaz area, where money is in extensive circulation, give coins or small currency notes as gifts, usually 10 to 20 afghanis, sometimes more depending on the wealth and intimacy of the visitor and hostess. The Hazara women of the highlands, where cash is scarce, give fried breads as favors. These gifts are terminologically distinguished according to the occasion: when a child is born or a new house completed or a kinsman has returned after a long absence, they are known as *shakarreyz,* "sugar-pouring"; when someone has returned from the hospital, as *khayraat-e-sar,* "offering for the head"; when someone has died or is marrying, as *destarkhaan* (which otherwise means a cloth on which food is served).

Petty gifts among the women and food among the men are considered loans to be reciprocated at a later time. A woman for instance, will remember for many years what each woman gave her at a certain occasion, no matter how large the gathering may have been. When the opportunity arises, one must pay out an equivalent amount in gifts to his creditors, ideally a bit more. If not, the offended creditors will gossip about him, and eventually refuse to go to his house or assist him in a time of need. Or sometimes, they send messages demanding payment, or clarification on why their gift was never reciprocated.

Obligations are inherited like debts. A son (or a brother, if the son is small and the brothers have not divided the inheritance) inherits a man's obligations as well as his financial debts. A daughter (if she has not married out) or a son's wife (if the daughter has) inherits a woman's obligations. The credit for having sponsored a feast or given a gift is inherited in the same way, i.e., to the son (or brother) of a male, to a son's wife (or daughter) of a female.

Besides drawing all kinsmen generally into relationships of mutual obligation, the feasts and gifts draw nearer relatives especially close because the close kinsmen often have to loan some of the resources necessary to give the feast or gift. The cost of a woman's gift to an outsider, for example, is shared by her close female relatives, those in her household and those who have married out of it. Similarly, when a man sponsors a feast, his close relatives may contribute something for the feast, e.g., a sheep, goat, even a cow, or sometimes cash. He should publicly acknowledge these contributions and say something complimentary about them, e.g., "It was very fat, a valuable animal," "He went to a lot of expense."

Most of these gifts are supposed to be reciprocated at a later date though sometimes a smaller gift, e.g., a kid or lamb, is given by a close relative without an expectation of direct return. In addition, the host is expected to give his donors some personal gifts at the time of the feast. For example, a man gave an especially large marriage feast for his son in which he expended 80,000 afghanis, some of it borrowed from eight closely related families. Each of them also contributed a goat or 500 afghanis. Besides inviting every member of his sect in his neighborhood he also invited 25 relatives living in Kabul. He fed his Kabul visitors for 15 days and gave each a cloak (*chapan*). To each of the families who contributed to his feast he gave a cloak. In addition, he should also contribute to each of them a goat when they sponsor a wedding feast. In return, he will then receive a cloak from them.

A man's affines also may contribute to his feast, but these gifts are more promptly and equally reciprocated. After the feast they are given gifts deemed equivalent to what they brought. They are calculated, for example, as follows:

> We think maybe his sheep is worth 500 afghanis, and his rice 300 afghanis—altogether 800 afghanis. He has a wife, and two or three sons, one or two daughters and himself, who will be eating the feast. So we figure we will owe him something. So when he leaves we will give him a cloak and his wife and daughters some clothes. And when we serve the meal, we say "So-and-so brought such-and-such," and this makes them happy.

Kinsmen should loan goods or cash to each other in times of need. When a farmer's stores of flour are used up before harvest, his kinsmen may loan him some until his crop comes in. When an unexpected visitor arrives they may have to loan him sugar or tea, which in the highlands are scarce. In a crisis involving a dispute they may loan him cash.

Obtaining cash loans, however, even among close kinsmen, is nowadays rather difficult, probably because of a general decline in the economy. A person may ask a wealthy kinsman for a small loan, but nowadays, to get it, he must have an especially good reputation; and if given, the loan must be repaid rather promptly. A short-term loan from a close relative is usually given without interest, but a long-term loan almost always brings high interest.

## The Obligation to Help

Kinsmen are also obliged to help each other when asked. There are many situations in which a person may need help. If his bull or donkey is lost on the mountains he may ask his relatives to help search for it. If constructing a new house or an additional room, he may request their help for the non-specialized chores. In a personal disaster, such as the collapse of a ceiling after a heavy rain, or a personal injury or sickness, he may request help.

The kinsmen are supposed to help, if asked. It is understood that sometimes a relative may be unable to help at a particular time, but if he persistently neglects to help when asked, he may in return fail to get help when he needs it. An unhelpful kinsman can be cut off from fellowship with the rest. "No one would come to see him at an Id festival or at a wedding in his family and this would embarrass him." Moreover, should he become involved in a dispute, his kinsmen would not support him.

A man will not usually ask non-relatives for labor assistance. Kinsmen help because they recognize a common fund of obligation from which they also need to draw, but non-kin do not. If a person needs help where he has no kinsman, he may be in difficulty. A man, for instance, who had brought a load of trees on donkeys down to the main road, had to unload his animals alone because there was no qawmi around to help him. He struggled by himself as others watched.

An acquaintance once said to me, "If a qawm member kills you, at least he will pull you into the shade." A qawm member is supposed to be at least more helpful—however he may feel about you personally—than a non-qawmi.

For special projects, such as building a house, a man will invite many kinsmen to come help him and during the period of the project will provide their noon meals. This is known as doing *aashur.* One man, for example, spent three summer seasons building a house on a hill overlooking his land. He had three hired workers but also several times called for his relatives—his "qawmi," he said—to help him. He went around and asked all the members of his qawm community and all affinal qawm communities in the valleys and neighboring valleys. He did not approach members of the opposing sect living nearby. The ones who came, came out of friendship, he said. Besides the hired laborers and the carpenters, 10 to 12 qawmi took turns every two or three days constructing adobe walls and mud floors and excavating the mountain side. His wife prepared feasts for about 20 people each day.

The political leaders (mirs and arbaabs) representing the people to the government do aashur to get their harvesting or plowing done, for most of them are too busy with political affairs to do their own work. Weak political patrons are unable to draw much aashur help and so must usually do most of their own work. Strong leaders, however, can maintain the ties of reciprocal help through doing political favors for their kinsman-clients and by giving feasts. A strong leader's prestige may be such as to attract, besides his own qawmi, some other "friends" (i.e., clients) from other qawmi communities, but actually, it is said, one can only require aashur help from one's own kinsmen. Mirs and other wealthy persons usually also have hired hands. These, I was told, work harder than the voluntary helpers.

## GENEROSITY AND PRESTIGE IN THE KINSHIP NETWORK

The idiom, then, of social fellowship in both circles of exchange is reciprocal generosity. Generous giving is the means by which a person gains a position of respect, a "name," among his kinsmen. There are other ways of building a good reputation—e.g., holding a respected position in government or reciting well the Quran or other poetry—but for most persons a good name is gained through generosity in feast-sponsoring and gift-giving.

The obligations of sharing tend to converge on the wealthy, who can afford to be more generous than the others. A man's wealth is described in terms of generosity, as in this statement:

> He is famous for his wealth, for his generosity and the number of visitors and servants eating in his house every day. Sometimes he has a

> hundred people for dinner; he will take in anyone for dinner. There is no one like him in all of Bamian. He owns maybe a hundred *kharwaar*[1] of land and two or three flour mills and maybe 1,000,000 trees and three cars. Sometimes people can borrow one of the cars for their own use.

Besides being much respected in their local kinship networks, the wealthy are influential among government officials. Sometimes they become guarantors for persons held for trial, and sometimes, by giving favors, win for them a favorable decision in court. It is said of a rich man, "People see his face."

The merging of concepts of wealth and influence is evident in certain vernacular terms. A *naamdaar*, "name-haver," is a prestigious person, and by extension a wealthy one. The adjective *motabar*, generally translated "wealthy," also means (in this region) "powerful": e.g., "The governor is very motabar because he can tell the judge what to do and he has to do it."[2] To be motabar is to be both rich and influential.

A *khaanawaada* (= *Khaan* = *Saayeb-e-rosokh*) is a man of very great wealth and influence, such as the one described in the quote above. A khaanawaada is a category of relative eminence. In Tagaw, especially in the markaz area, where there is a greater concentration of wealth, sometimes there are more than one khaanawaada in a qawm community; but in the highlands, which are poorer, there are relatively few khaanawaadas. Similarly, a khaanawaada's kinsmen are variously reckoned: the wealthier he is, the wider is his set of kinship connections. He sometimes refers to the members of his kinship set as his qawmi.

Geographically close khaanawaadas may compete with each other for the loyalty of weaker kinsmen by inviting them to their houses. In addition to the gatherings after the Friday prayers, they may simply invite them to come over informally to discuss current issues in the community. Such gatherings serve the interest of a khaanawaada because by providing the food he wins the loyalty of his guests, and by consulting with them on current issues he stays abreast of current opinion. Such meetings also serve the interests of his weaker kinsmen, for they enable them to express their respect for the khaanawaada and maintain a relationship with him which could in a time of need be the basis for his support.

Local factions tend to polarize around khaanawaadas. Where there are more than one khaanawaada in a small area, persons may be more loyal to one than to another, but will give respect to both. But if the tension between the two khaanawaadas becomes overt hostility, the weaker persons have to line up solidly for one against the other. A khaanawaada will speak of those who are loyal as his "good friends" or his "good qawmi."

[1] A *kharwaar* is 1,246 pounds. This is the amount of seed used in planting his land. The actual area depends on the quality of the soil.

[2] This statement is actually incorrect under the new constitution, but it illustrates the usage.

## TENSION IN THE KINSHIP NETWORK

### Hoarding and Sharing

In the system of reciprocal sharing among kinsmen there is an underlying problem: People may want to share for social reasons but to survive they must be personally acquisitive. With a narrow margin of subsistence the peasants cannot afford to share too liberally although they must appear generous. As goods are scarce, there is a tension between the value of a good name through sharing and the personal necessity to hoard. Consequently, everyone hoards secretly while publicly pretending to share as liberally as his limited means will allow.

The practical importance of sharing and cooperating, rather than enhancing feelings of fellowship and intimacy, tends to breed suspicion and hostility. In the exchange of goods and services givers and receivers evaluate the amounts exchanged differently. Givers of course tend to overestimate and receivers to underestimate the values of contributions. At a feast one's guests frequently seem ungrateful and insufficiently aware of their obligation. Indeed, the host may be suspected of being niggardly in expenditures for a feast, so instead of gaining prestige he loses it. "We spend our money and our name turns bad anyway," complained one informant. To avoid such a loss a host goes to great efforts to ensure that his feasts are sumptuous. He would be publicly embarrassed if the food were not abundantly more than the guests could consume. Fortunately, the intricacy of reciprocal obligations restrains excessive criticism.

That the obligation to share is enforced by social pressure is implied in the private techniques employed to evade it. Individuals hoard their private goods from sight. Adult members of a household keep storage boxes in which they lock their few private possessions. To avoid having to share goods which I gave them, people often hid the gifts and did not acknowledge them publicly (though of course they did privately) unless circumstances absolutely required it.

### Gossip and Scandal as Mechanisms of Social Control

What then enforces the practice of reciprocal sharing? As already stated, the mutual need for support constrains people to help and give as required. In addition, two other forces operate to maintain reciprocity: gossip and scandal.[3]

[3]The terms gossip and scandal are used here in the sense which I take to be Gluckman's in his article on this subject. The following quotes suggest his intent, and mine. "Makah gossip does not show merely that general interest in the doings, and the virtues and vices, of others, which characterizes any group. The gossip passes beyond this state and becomes vicious scandal, aimed at demonstrating that the other parties are not worthy. . . " (1963:311). "It is good manners to gossip and scandalize about your dearest friends with those who belong, even though it be their dearest friends—but it is bad manners . . . to tell unpleasant stories about your friends to strangers" (*Ibid.:* 313).

Gossip and scandal mobilize public opinion against persons who do not share fairly.

Moral evaluations of the behavior of others pervade social interaction. Such evaluations assume a supreme standard for all moral persons, namely fairness. Gluckman has pointed out that

> The values of [a] group are clearly asserted in gossip and scandal, since a man or woman is always run down for failing to live up to these values (1963:312).

When groups are together talking about incidents in their daily routines or incidents heard from others, they express their opinion of people's behavior, censoring or approving according to their conceptions or fairness. An example is the following incident, recounted to me by an elderly highlander.

> To show you what those people [on the Tagaw] are like, one time in winter I was on my way to Bamian [i.e., to the markaz from his provincial village], and when it began to get dark I had to stop. It was very cold and the snow was deep. So I stopped in a village near the road and went to the mosque to stay for the night. It was, I admit, warm there. But while I was trying to get warm and wondering how I was to get food, someone came along and asked me what I was doing there. I said I was on my way to Bamian but it was cold and dark and also dangerous, since the wolves would be out at night, so I had to stop somewhere and I came to the mosque to spend the night. Then I asked for food but no one did anything for me. Later, two soldiers came in and those people treated them unfriendly too, as they had me. Finally much later the mullah of the mosque came in and I told him my story—how I had come there because I could go no further, and I didn't have anything to eat but would gladly pay something if I could get it, etc., but no one around there would be nice to me; they gave me no food, no blanket, hardly even a "hello."
>
> Well, that mullah would not let those people get by with that: He made them cook food for me. So finally after a long time a bountiful meal was brought to me. Of course, then they wouldn't take any money for it. It was a good meal, but it was because the mullah interceded on my behalf. A little later someone fed the soldiers too, and they offered some of their meal to me, but I was so full, I couldn't accept. So finally I got plenty to eat. But, you see, that's how they treat travelers down there. In our place a traveler would never be treated that way. . . .

The incident he related, like so many in anyone's life, reveals certain characteristics of people's behavior which can be judged by a moral standard. In telling the incident he invoked fairness as the standard of acceptable morality in others, and by implication affirmed it as the standard for all.

The opinion of the adults dominating the kinship network is the sustaining force for the good reputations of various individuals. A man's reputation is built up by talk of his generosity and fairness; it is diminished by talk of his miserliness and acquisitiveness. As gossip is not static, the reputations or "names" of personages over time gradually shift with respect to each other, some persons becoming more esteemed, others less so. Consequently, when kinsmen meet together, they test each other so as to assess their own current statuses. A man, for example, may tease his kinsman by suggesting that he plans to ask them for something, usually an unreasonable demand. Their response displays their willingness to comply, and by implication their respect for him.

People also attempt to constrain others to reciprocate more generously by exaggerating the ability of others to repay their debts in generous amounts. Said one person of another sitting in the group, "The worst clothes are worn by the richest people in order to avoid paying their fair share. Habib is actually very well off, but he wants to act poor." Habib was actually poor, but the speaker was reminding him that his debts should be repaid in full.

The need of kinsmen for each other usually sets limits on how keenly a man may chide his kinsmen, and also on how irritable they may be in response to his chiding. If his teasing is too caustic, they could wholly withdraw from his fellowship and deprive him of needful assistance. But they dare not be overtly irritable at such teasing, lest they similarly lose a useful ally. The poor have to bear more chiding than the wealthy, because they have more need of the richer man's help than he of theirs. The poor, as a result, often endure more coarse chiding and rough, condescending treatment.

To avoid becoming vulnerable to gossip and scandal people shroud their personal affairs in secrecy. Usages of the word *parda,* "curtain, veil, cover," express the value of personal secrecy to maintain self respect. *Parda kardan* means "to veil" or "to hide," and implies modesty in social relations. It is said, for example, *shooleyt-a-boxo, paradeyt-a-buko,* "Eat your pudding and draw your curtain," i.e., tend to your own business. *Pardey-mardum-a-bokoo ke khodaa pardeyt-a-bokona,* "Hide other people's faults so that God will hide yours." To be *beyparda* "without curtain," is to be embarrassed. A person who attempts to gloss over the faults of others is "doing *parda.*" It therefore implies a sense of pride and self respect: *maa az xod aab-o-parda daareym,* "We have our own water and curtain," i.e., we have a source of self respect of our own (a respectable background).

Secrecy concerning one's personal affairs is a means of protection. Information given to enemies can be used against one to injure his reputation in the community, as a kind of weapon. Divulging information about one's self involves an amount of risk, and complete, wholly accurate personal information is not given to persons who are not trusted friends.

Information is sometimes distorted when given to outsiders. In my initial contacts with people they often distorted information. Once, for example, in a tea shop I casually asked a traveler what he was doing there and he answered that he was selling rugs (*gelams*). Later I overheard him explaining to another person (of his own ethnic group) that he had come to buy (not sell) rugs. Another time, while staying in a home, I asked someone if he ever had difficulties with the nomads. He said, no, they never caused any problem. Soon afterward, an elder came into the room, vouched for my trustworthiness, and encouraged the others to give whatever information I needed for my research. Then the kinsmen corrected his earlier statement: the nomads had, he said, been quite a lot of trouble to him; and he described some difficulties he had personally experienced.

Moreover, information about specific tensions and difficulties among close kinsmen had to be obtained from individuals when alone, sometimes only after they were assured that specific details would not be exposed to others in their group. People who freely chatted individually about local problems changed the subject when others entered the room.

The practice of secrecy among kinsmen, rather than effectively reducing the transfer of news, seems to heighten the inquisitiveness, rumor, and suspicion. People understand each other's subtle evasions only too well, so suspicion pervades their social interaction. Many seem concerned about losing their fair share, or being cheated by secret alliances. As a result, any obvious advantage a man has can be resented by envious neighbors. A man with an exceptionally productive milch-cow, or a specially fertile field, for instance, has something to fear: people will talk about it. Envious and fearful kinsmen may resent other blessings as well, e.g., a pretty wife, or a healthy brood of children. Thus, a man fears for what benefits he has, lest envy injure him and destroy his advantage.

Gossip and scandal mobilize the envy and suspicion between kinsmen so as to bring their opinion to bear upon each other. If one does not share, or shows himself unfair or avaricious, they will talk. And the talk will destroy his social image. This is especially true among the closely bound kinsmen of a qawm community. In the qawm community everyone knows everyone else. They live next to each other all their lives, whether they like each other personally or not. Because they are dependent on a stationary capital asset, land, they cannot move away from their neighbors. Similarly, from the gossip and scandal of their neighbors there is no hiding place. One does not easily live down a bad name. If malicious talk begins, it can continue for years; gossip can chain a man to an ugly image for life. On the other hand, gossip can be rewarding to a generous man; a man with a good name may be able for a while to take advantage of the crest of a good name among his kinsmen, exploiting their good faith without fully repaying his obligation, though of course not indefinitely.

People remember the times when they came into conflict before, and they learn to invoke these past irritations when they are angry and to forget them when in fellowship. So hostilities tend to resonate between kinsmen, just as their relationship ties reduplicate. When hostilities build up, a person may be tempted to leave the community, but as this of course would also entail leaving his land, he cannot afford to move. He is held close to his kinsmen by necessity, even though toward some of them he may harbor deep-seated hostility.

## FISSIVE AND FUSIVE PROCESSES IN SOCIAL RELATIONS

The description of the social system in this and the previous chapter indicates that inherent in the relations drawing persons into groups are tensions that could force them apart. At every level of typological inclusiveness divisive as well as cohesive tendencies exist. Tensions in the conjugal bond, besides ruining the happiness of the family, can disrupt social arrangements at higher levels. Tensions among the women of a household can endanger its unity. Tensions over land in the qawm community can bring its members into conflict. Tensions in the kinship network engender suspicion and envy.

This description, then, reveals a set of contrary tensions inherent in the social system: social groups can fly apart almost as easily as they can hold together. Both divided forms and cohesive forms of social groupsing can exist in Bamian. Cohesion can appear at the several levels of social grouping: the family, the household, the qawm community, the neighborhood, and the kinship network. Division, in contrast, seldom appears in the family, though conjugal tensions may breed strains that ramify elsewhere. But division may appear at the other levels of social grouping: in the household, as the women of the household, and sometimes the men, become antagonistic over work habits or violations of sexual rights; in the qawm community, as the qawmi who share a canal are drawn into conflict over boundary crowding; in the kinship network, as kinsmen who are supposed to share, feeling victimized by the acquisitiveness of relatives, realign themselves against each other.

Since the social system inherently embodies contrary social tensions, it is susceptible to any divisive or cohesive influences imposed upon it by environmental conditions. Where the environment strongly favors the cohesion of social groups, the groups, though enshrouding internal hostilities, will appear solidary. Where the environment imposes only loose constraints on social groups, they may, when internecine antagonisms arise, fall apart. The divisive tendencies extant everywhere in Bamian are manifest in Shibar as broken qawm communities. The cohesive forces extant everywhere in the area are manifest as solidary communities in the other regions of Bamian. The design presented here is one of fissive processes and fusive processes operating in relative balance to bring about united or divided communities in Bamian. Chapter V attempts to explain how the fissive processes become expressed as religious conversion.

So far, we have only suggested why qawm communities should fly apart. One of the possible causes for division in qawm communities, i.e., disputes over dike-crowding, may also be a reason for the checkered social alignments in neighborhoods in Shibar and Kalu. In this chessboard of factions adjacent qawm communities in neighborhoods are at odds with each other. No specific cases were discovered of inter-qawm community conflict over common dikes, but it seems reasonable to suppose that the tensions between persons over their dikes may affect relations between adjacent qawm communities. As already noted, the populations of neighborhoods are only loosely united, but the members of qawm communities are relatively solidary. Where the irrigated plots of qawm community members ajoin the plots of members of other qawm communities, their tensions over the delimiting dikes are not molified by strong bonds of unity such as those among members of a qawm community; consequently, any dispute over a dike separating their plots may more easily rupture their social relations. Moreover, a land dispute between two such persons is likely to draw to each the support of his respective qawmi. Thus, neighboring qawm communities can easily become aligned against each other in territorial disputes.

It is possible that the tension over adjacent territories follows a pattern similar to that of nomadic tribes in south Persia (Barth, 1961:130), where adjacent tribes line up against each other, but alternate tribes, as each pair has a common adversary, align in loose confederations. Possibly, the checkered alignment of sectarian groups in parts of Shibar and Kalu is a result of a similar opposition of groups over abutting territories. Chapter VI will argue that this pattern of alternate oppositions in Kalu and Shibar takes the overt form of sectarian factions because in this area feuding communities have the option of aligning themselves with larger orders of political antagonism, i.e., the two sects, Ismailism and Imamism.

# V

# SOCIAL SYSTEM III: COMMUNITY FISSION

UP TO this point the discussion of fissive tendencies within kinship groups has implied that the only manifestation of these fissive tendencies is the sectarian chessboard in Shibar. Actually, division occurs among kinsmen everywhere in Bamian, but only in Shibar does it take shape as a sectarian division. This chapter describes the processes of qawm community fission: the general pattern of fission, in which a defeated disputant emigrates from the community; and the pattern seemingly peculiar to Shibar, in which a defeated disputant converts to a different religious sect.

## THE POWER OF COMMUNITY CONSENSUS

As explained earlier, the ties of solidarity between qawm community members, whatever their emotional sentiments, are powerful. Qawmi are functionally united through their common dependence on an irrigation canal, their mutual help arrangements, their intricate ties of descent and affinity, and their associated patterns of reciprocal sharing. Moreover, they tend to conceptually merge their notions of kinship closeness, political solidarity, religious unity, and territorial grouping into a single concept, the kinship-based qawm community. An outright dispute between qawmi threatens these economic and social ties and therefore is usually sanctioned by the community.

Community consensus is usually the decisive factor in the outcome of a dispute. A disputing person who persistently refuses to accept a solution suggested by the community elders is in danger of losing their economic and political support, which in an exigency are vital for his survival. Even if he were to flout their opinion and appeal to the government court, he would still likely need them as witnesses on his behalf and perhaps also as sources of financial aid. In a quarrel, then, he must primarily maneuver to win their political backing.

Thus, a disputant, unless he is especially powerful, is usually forced to acquiesce to the majority opinion.

> There was a young man [for instance] who had two sisters, one of marriageable age, but no other relatives. He was poor, owning only a small parcel of land. He made an agreement to give his older sister in marriage to a man of a neighboring qawm community in exchange for the man's daughter. The sister was given in marriage to the man first. However, when the boy asked for the man's daughter in return, he was initially told that she was sick, but later that the girl did not want him. The father of the girl, to ensure that she would not have to marry the boy, took her to the seat of government to swear to an official that she did not want the boy. This shocked everyone.
>
> The boy therefore began to talk about initiating a legal suit against the man. But eventually the leaders of the two communities were able to work out a settlement in which the girl's father would pay the boy 9,000 afghanis and sponsor a feast for him. The young man, though forced to accept this settlement, was dissatisfied because the cost of a bride was much greater than this remuneration. He announced at the dinner that he would not really accept this settlement. As he had given his sister, he wanted a wife—no money, only a girl. He made sure that a lot of his qawmi were at the feast so that his host would not later deny what he had said. For him the matter was not really settled, even though he had been obliged to consent to the will of the elders.

This kind of situation can be the source of enduring personal animosities which fester to more serious proportions, but for the immediate crisis the elders had been able to control the dispute by working out a settlement which they could impose upon the two parties. They succeeded in avoiding government involvement and consequently saved both sides from the great costs of an official case. Furthermore, despite the persistence of ill-feeling between the two parties, they were still held within their respective communities.

## FISSION BY EMIGRATION

There are three alternatives for a person who has not been satisfactorily supported by his community in a dispute: either he must acquiesce to the majority opinion, as in the case above; or he must physically remove himself from the group, perhaps with the possibility of an eventual rapprochement; or under certain circumstances, he may remain in the community but become realigned to another group through conversion. In the last two cases, he chooses to break socially from his qawmi rather than consent to their opinion. His division from his group under such circumstances has economic and political consequences, for by losing fellowship with the rest of his community, he is cut away from the supportive and cooperative ties important for his status and vital for his livelihood.

> There were three sisters [for example] who had no surviving brothers, and so were the heiresses of their father's land. One of the sisters died, however, after bearing a son, and her land was divided between the two other sisters. When the son of the deceased sister became old enough to understand that some of the land was legally his, he pressed his maternal aunts for his land, but got no satisfaction. Eventually, without consulting the leaders of his qawm community, he went directly to the government with his complaint. This caused a lot of ill-feeling among his local qawmi, but the elders avoided a court case by forcing the young man to accept a cash payment and a portion of the land he claimed from his aunts. He was constrained by the entire community to accept the land and money, but he felt he should have received more. Eventually he again went to the government to complain. This time also one of the elders intervened before the case became officially registered, and provided the necessary evidence to convince the local officials that the sisters had already made a settlement for the land. The young man's second complaint to the government, however, alienated him from his kinsmen, and having no hope of gaining their support, he left the community and went to Kabul.

The boy is not likely to soon reestablish close ties with his kinsmen, for both they and he have no desire to renew contact. The boy now has lost the political and economic support of his kinsmen and may never regain it. He has been functionally cut off from his natal kinship group. (Of course, not all social breaks of this kind are so permanent as this one. Very commonly, close relatives fight over property but eventually are reconciled and return to normal expressions of kinship cooperation.)

A person may win a dispute in court and still be forced out of the community.

> After the death of an elderly neighbor [for example] Khayr Maamad claimed that a piece of land being cultivated by a son of the deceased was actually his, because, said he, the deceased neighbor had for some years been encroaching onto Khayr Maamad's property. The entire community disagreed with him, but he took the claim to court anyway. The court also rejected his claim, but allowed him the option, legally recognized in Islam, of swearing on the Quran that the young man's claim to the disputed plot was false. Though all his kinsmen and even the government officials believed he was lying, they were willing to accept this procedure as binding, expecting God to directly inflict him with a serious punishment.
>
> Khayr Maamad was legally awarded the land, but back in his village the young man still refused to hand it over. Finally, Khayr Maamad beat him up and by force took possession of it. The community, however, was so incensed against Khayr Maamad that he soon decided to leave. He rented out his land and moved to Kabul.

A person at odds with his qawmi is prudent to move out because the community can turn against him in a time of crisis. The case of Hosayn Ali may be an example:

> Hosayn Ali sold some land to his Saint, an eminent religious authority named Sayyed Aliyawar, residing in another district. According to the earlier practice, the sale was only registered with the local mir. Years later, after the government began recording transactions, Hosayn Ali claimed that the money was never paid. As the sale had not been registered with the government, he won his case in court. He was therefore paid the money a second time, but of course he had become permanently estranged from Sayyed Aliyawar. More seriously, he lost the confidence of his own kinsmen, who besides disapproving of Hosayn Ali's dishonesty, regarded Sayyed Aliyawar as a Saint.
>
> Some time later Sayyed Aliyawar became involved in a dispute with another Saint. Hosayn Ali's qawm community of course sided with Sayyed Aliyawar, but Hosayn Ali, unable to conciliate with Sayyed Aliyawar, further isolated himself from his kinsmen by declaring himself for the opposing Saint. Hosayn Ali's position was now doubly precarious. He had on account of the first incident lost the confidence of his qawmi and on account of the second had made himself their opponent in a major dispute.
>
> The dispute grew in acrimony and involved a number of charges and counter charges implicating almost everyone in the area. During a period of intense feeling Hosayn Ali's wife fell into a bitter argument with a neighbor woman, the wife of one of his awdurzaadas (FaBrSo), and later the same day Hosayn Ali himself became involved. Soon afterwards the neighbor woman died, presumably from a wound inflicted in the argument. Under other circumstances, the woman's death might have been reported only as a natural death and the claims against Hosayn Ali, if any, would have been settled within the community. But the feeling against Hosayn Ali was now so strong that the elders of the qawm community themselves accused him of murder in the government court.
>
> The followings of the two opposing Saints sided with the two parties in the murder case, so the dispute between Hosayn Ali and his kinsmen became a test of the relative strengths of the two religious blocs. One side claimed the woman had died of an accidental fall and the other claimed she had been deliberately killed. Eventually, the court decided Hosayn Ali was guilty and sentenced him to prison. As already noted, however, had Hosayn Ali been on good terms with his kinsmen the case would likely have been settled out of court.

Persons may at one time have been able to remove themselves from their kinsmen by relocating to another locality nearby. In the valley of Labmushak

(Fig. 7) the spatial distribution of descent groups suggests that persons have in the past split off from parent stems. Groups recognizing a rather close line of kinship sometimes occupy distant territories. In some instances it seems clear that one or more families have gone to the trouble of relocating only a few hundred yards away from their natal qawm community. Actual instances of this kind of hiving off from a parent community, however, were not found, so it can only be conjectured that one reason for the spatial scattering of kinship groups was internal tension.

## RELIGIOUS CONVERSION

Defeated persons emigrate from their natal communities everywhere in Bamian, including Shibar, and as a consequence most of their qawm communities maintain an appearance of homogeneity and strong solidarity. In the valleys of Shibar, however, a dissident person has another option which, though involving dissolution of ties with close qawmi, still enables him to remain on his land. This is the option of religious conversion. Religious conversion, as described earlier, has fractured some qawm communities in Shibar. Internecine disputes have eventuated in a drastic reformulation of the disputants' kinship, political and religious connections, and the ostracized individuals have become, so to speak, socially different persons.

In a quote in Chapter I, one person denied that conversion was possible (see p. 9). He argued that the practical difficulties of conversion were insurmountable. If someone were to convert, he would lose the support of everyone in his community as well as of his Saint and of his mullah, and so he could not really remain in the community. The statement, while aiming to say that conversion was impossible because it was impractical, leaves unclear whether conversion is possible for a person already hopelessly out of fellowship with his kinsmen.

The denials quoted earlier notwithstanding, certain informants clearly indicated that persons have, albeit rarely, converted in Shibar. An instance of conversion in an originally Ismaili family was described by one informant as follows:

> Three brothers shared as they should, but when they died their families fought over the inheritance. Eventually they split up both spatially and religiously. They divided into the three sects—Sunni, Imami and Ismaili. One of these families, the Sunni, was unable to get along in our district because the others wouldn't tolerate a Sunni, so his family left. The other two families stayed.

No further details were obtained on the circumstances of this family quarrel but it seems apparent that the "conversions" were maneuvers associated with attempts to gain leverage in the struggle for the inheritance. In this case, as the conflict between the families had become so intense that no hope of reconciliation remained, it apparently was feasible, perhaps even necessary, for the opposing sides to align themselves with the larger social blocs, the sects.

What progression of social realignments could have led to such a break? I have no complete case history of a conversion. Instead, there is merely evidence that conversions have taken place, and incomplete hints of conversion, such as the description above. A model of the behavior of quarrelling qawmi is therefore proposed which indicates how conversion could have taken place and resulted in the fractionated community structure peculiar to Shibar. The model is abstracted from fragmentary information obtained from the few informants who would discuss such events and from the social system already described. The model is as follows:

A dispute of some vital importance, such as a conflict over land, develops between two families in a qawm community. The argument continues for some time. The families break off all social activities and begin to slander each other among their kinsmen. Eventually, the elders of the qawm community, attempting a reconciliation, work out a solution, but one of the sides, feeling slighted, refuses to accept it. The dissenting family, as it becomes hostile toward its entire qawm community, is faced with the characteristic alternative: either to get out of the community and probably lose the disputed territory, or to stay on the land and attempt to form new cooperative-sharing ties with other groups in the neighborhood. To be able to take the second alternative, the family must be situated in the following circumstances: (1) As suggested earlier, it must live where economic cooperation with its neighbors is not vital for survival. That is, it must have rainfall lands on which it depends to a relatively great degree, and its irrigated lands must be close to a well-supplied, natural water flow, so that the family can, if necessary, dig a private canal. (2) It must live near members of the other sect, for in times of economic and political crisis, it must have other social ties outside its natal community. The need for political backing during a dispute is of course great because the new connections must be formed as the conflict intensifies. Such new social ties can only be formed with a group willing to accept the dissident family and dwelling near enough to help and share with it.

Certain localities of Shibar, as described earlier, provide these circumstances. In Shibar irrigation water sharing is relatively less important, and in places the natural water flow is more than abundant; also, the two hostile sects, Ismailis and Imamis, dwell close together in many neighborhoods. Some neighborhoods of Shibar, then, do in fact provide a dissident family with the possibility of physically remaining on its territories without a disastrous economic and political collapse.

The new group to which the family attempts to align itself is one that can identify with the family's quarrel because, belonging to the opposite sect and being situated nearby, it probably has already had numerous conflicts over territorial boundaries with the members of that community. If the family disputing with the rest has previously had a good reputation, certain generous persons in the neighboring village may initially express sympathy for the family's cause. Moreover, their distrust of the other community, already heightened by the sectarian barrier, seems to be confirmed by the complaints of the disputing family. As a result, the neighbors, informally at first, identify with the cause of the one family.

New ties between the dissenting family and the neighboring group develop. At first they may only be evident informally as the disputing family complains to the others. Later, it helps someone in the other community during harvest or plowing season, and in return receives similar help. As it loses influence in its natal group, it prizes more dearly these ties to the neighboring community and attempts to develop them into protective and supportive bonds to undergird its socially tenuous position. Though these are, of course, first established by reciprocal cooperative and sharing contacts, they eventually are reinforced by intermarriage.

The disputing family thus gradually becomes socially aligned with a neighboring community which, as noted earlier, belongs to the contrary religious bloc. This change in allegiance is, of course, short of religious conversion: few people adjust their ideological convictions as easily as they change friends. The family probably still maintains connections with the Saint of the natal community and affirms its belief in the doctrines of its sect. But its relationship to the sect and the Saint are affected by its new social alignment. Its religious connections become less important as distinguishing marks of its social identity. Indeed its sectarian beliefs suggest an embarrassing dissonance with the very group of persons to whom it is now somewhat tenuously aligned. Also, its status with its Saint is being undermined, for while the family may continue to pay the Saint respect, he is nevertheless informed of the community dispute by other followers sympathetic to the position of the community opposing the family. Thus, the old ties of relationship to the Saint and the sect are gradually weakened by the new social status of the family.

At the same time, new religious influences are being exerted on the family through its new circle of sharing and helping. In public gatherings the family comes to know the religious authorities of the contrary sect. And from its new friends it hears good things about their Saint. Moreover, the doctrines of the contrary sect are presented in a more favorable light than the family had encountered earlier.

Thus, if the family's ties persist with the neighboring community, the family or its offspring will eventually become identified with the Saint and the sect of its new friends. Its animosity toward the natal community, expressed earlier as accusations of dishonesty and immorality, merely becomes part of the body of suspicion and derogatory myth about the members of the other sect in general.

This is the form of conversion whereby a family turns to neighboring hostile groups for support in a quarrel against its own natal community. The family converts either from Ismailism to Imamism or vice versa, depending on its original status. A family converting from either of these sects to Sunnism must employ different tactics because Sunni groups are not interspersed among the other two. A family who, rather than leaning toward its neighbors, turns to the government for support against its qawmi is in fact turning to a Sunni institution for leverage. A second scheme, then, may be advanced to suggest the pattern of conversion leading to Sunnism: a dissident family, in order to win its case in a Sunni court, aligns itself to Sunni families well connected with government, and eventually declares itself to be Sunni.

The possibility of such a measure for most Imamis or Ismailis is slight, but a few families of wealth and influence have been able to make this kind of identity change. Wealthy families often have connections with prominent Sunni families anyway, primarily economic ones, but sometimes they also have kinship ties, for occasionally an Ismaili or Imami Hazara bride is given to a wealthy Sunni.

Only one case is known of the conversion of a Hazara to Sunnism, which is as follows:

> A wealthy man died rather suddenly in middle age and was survived by three small sons, and a younger brother. The brother, their uncle, took control of the entire estate, but to the children of the deceased when they grew up, he gave large amounts of land. He did not, however, divide the propery according to the ideal patterns of inheritance.
>
> The uncle through the years developed from this estate an immense wealth through multiple and diverse investments. He became so influential that for many years none of his three nephews, the sons who had a right to his estate, dared challenge him. Two of the three sons died and only the youngest son of the original owner lived to full adulthood. The uncle held the estate for many years, and it was evident that his own sons expected to inherit it when he died. The uncle came under pressure from the government for other reasons and the surviving son of the original owner took the opportunity to challenge his right to the estate. For some time the son was unsuccessful. Through his own sizable wealth and connections, however, he was eventually able to establish social connections with a leading religious family in another district. The family was Sunni and, besides being influential in religious circles, had connections with certain leading officials in his district.
>
> Eventually the son became engaged to a woman from the Sunni family. In a better position to obtain greater notice with the government officials of his district, he again made a formal complaint against his uncle, this

time at a higher echelon of government. He succeeded in creating a serious and complicated court case. It was during the involved investigations of this case that he identified himself as a Sunni. This of course was the decisive, final break with his natal family. By espousing his new sect, he formalized the new base of political maneuver from which he was operating. He became a "Sunni" without being a "Tajik," but probably he (or at least his children) will someday be known as Tajiks rather than Hazaras.

We have been concerned with how qawm communities are divided through internecine conflict. Qawm communities splinter either through the exodus of socially defeated persons from the community, or through their realignment to neighboring groups belonging to the opposing sect. To explain the second pattern it was assumed that in Shibar neighbors of the contrary sect already were dwelling close enough to the fissioning group to support them when they broke from the natal community. This does not, of course, explain how groups belonging to two opposing sects came in the first place to be together in Shibar, or why factional oppositions have to be formulated as religious differences. These issues are discussed in the next chapter.

# VI

# HISTORY AND POLITICAL PROCESSES

THE political history of Bamian discloses a differential in the degree to which outside political groups have influenced social relations within the basin. Whereas Tagaw has often been controlled by powerful groups outside Bamian, the highlands surrounding Tagaw have often been independent of outside control; the highland groups have, in fact, often been disunited among themselves. The eastern highlands of east-central Afghanistan seem in a special sense to be politically marginal, for this area lies at the frontiers of three historic centers of political power: Turkestan, Kabul, and Hazarajat (see Fig. 10). Moreover, the recent history of Bamian reveals the unity of political and religious identities, for the wars by which Abdul Rahman, the Amir of Kabul, brought the country under his control were fought between armies that had been mobilized mainly by religious appeals. These themes will be elaborated at the end of this chapter.

## HISTORY

### Ancient History

Very little is known about the differential in political influences across the Bamian landscape in ancient times. The ruins of ancient fortresses, most of them concentrated at either end of Tagaw, indicate Tagaw's political importance, while other ruins indicate the strategic significance of the lines of access leading into it. The ancient citadel of Gholghola, "The Noisy City," located at the mouth of the Kakrak valley, presides over the markaz area on the western end of Tagaw plain. Shari-i-Zohak, "The Red City," an ancient fortress famous in Persian epic poetry, is situated atop 350-foot cliffs overlooking the eastern end of Tagaw and its tributary valley, Paymuri. The importance of these locations derives from their control of the points where the trade routes converged within the valley.

> The importance of Bamian is therefore due to its position, as a [military] force located there would cover the group of passes . . . [around its

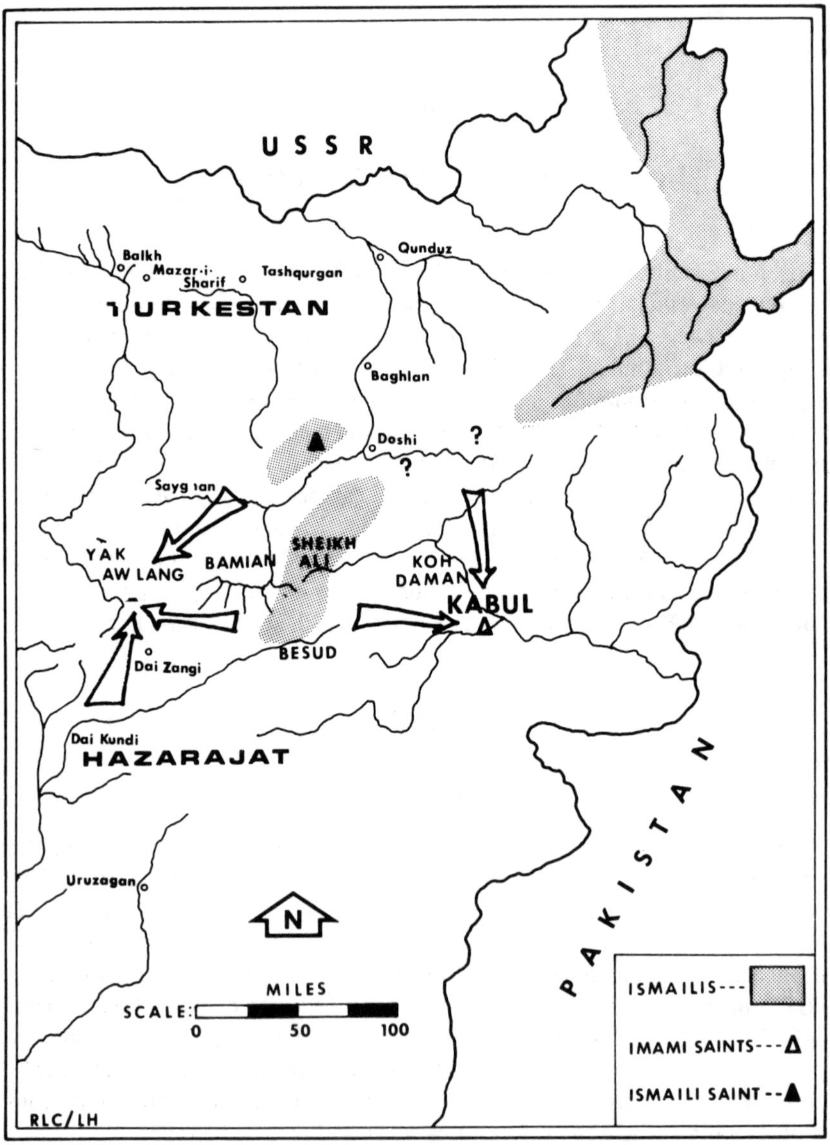


Figure 10. The historic centers of power in Bamian history.
Arrows point to catchment areas of Ismaili saints.

> perimeter] and would command the main route from Turkestan to the Afghan capital (Government of India, 1910:51).

Massive fortresses controlling the main historic lines of access into the Bamian basin are also located in the Shekari gorge, and in the valleys of Iraq (in Shibar), Jalmesh and Ghandak.

Bamian's strength in the ancient past was due to its geography: its strategic position and the qualities which made it a natural fortress. It lay along the major route of trade through the Hindu Kush mountains between the kingdoms of Central Asia to the north and those of India to the southeast. Trade between India and Bactria, and eventually China, passed through this basin.[1] The natural barriers surrounding it set easily defendable frontiers around it, and the fertile and expansive Tagaw plain ensured a stable source of agricultural products, adequate to support a strong rulership. As the basin was a natural fortress, economically self-sufficient, and strategically located along a route which in the seventh century had become a vital highway between the great civilizations of India and China, it flourished, especially in the markaz area, as a great cultural and political center.

Bamian's importance ended abruptly with its complete destruction by Ghengis Khan in the thirteenth century. It never regained its ancient strength, for the political rivalries and recurrent periods of political instability in Central Asia during the following 500 years atrophied the trade on which Bamian had thrived. The development of maritime traffic between Europe, India, and China brought the final and decisive blow to Bamian's eminent position. It has since been vulnerable to the powers who successively dominated either side of the Hindu Kush.

## Early Hazara Political Relations

The subsequent history of Bamian and central Afghanistan is only dimly known until about the fifteenth century. At this time three kinds of groups occupied this region: in the mountains south of the Hindu Kush there were tribes of Hazaras;[2] to the south and east of this region there were Afghan tribes; and to the north and west of the Hindu Kush range there were Turkic (Uzbek and Turkoman) groups.

The Hazaras, like many tribal groups where justice and revenge must be effected through vendetta, seemed constantly embroiled in feuds and internecine

[1] The following works provide the most detail on Bamian's ancient past: Godard, et al. (1928); Hackin and Hackin (1933); Hackin et al. (1959). N. Wolfe (1963) gives a readable summary in English.

[2] On the origin of the Hazaras of central Afghanistan, see Bacon, 1951.

raiding. Ferrier wrote what he had learned of them in the early half of the nineteenth century:

> They arm only for pillage, and no sovereign can reckon upon their following him into the field. . . . The Pusht Koh Hazarahs of Hassan Khan ben Zorab are constantly divided amongst themselves either by the intrigues of subaltern chiefs, or by family quarrels; they are always scheming and plotting one against the other . . . the Afghans always contrive to get through their [the Hazaras'] passes and attack them on their own ground, though they cannot occupy it permanently, and they content themselves with straining every nerve to get a good booty and be off again. By this constant hostility [there] is maintained such a lively hatred between the Afghans and the Hazarahs, that it is scarcely possible for the latter [= the Afghans?] to venture singly in the Paropamisus—a lonely traveller would assuredly be assassinated. He is obliged therefore to make a considerable circuit to go from Kabul to Herat, or vice versa, to accomplish a journey which would be so short if the country of the Hazarahs were safe. . . . Tamerlane seems to have been the last sovereign who subjugated the Hazarahs; they shook off the yoke at his death, and have remained free in their mountains ever since. The Sufaveans, the Grand Mogul, Nadir Shah, and Ahmed Shah Suddozye have never been able to subjugate them again. It appears that they have been the same from time immemorial. . . . (1857:220-221).

Among the Afghans the Hazaras were notorious for their incorrigibility. Amir Abdul Rahman said of them:

> The Hazaras had raided and plundered the neighboring subjects [of the Afghan confederacy] for about three hundred years past, and none of the kings had had the power to make them absolutely peaceful (Mir Munshi, 1900, Vol. I:279).[3]

Because of the incorrigibility of the Hazaras, traffic between Kabul and the north, which passed through Hazara territories, was often interrupted.

> Till about 70 years ago Hazarajat was very isolated, and in practice independent of the Central Government. At that time very few dared to go to Hazarajat; the nomads kept to the Pashtun area, and very few trade-caravans passed through the central parts, they preferred the route by the Unai, "Hajigak," and Iraq passes, to Bamian, and the more northern routes through the Sheikh Ali area in the Ghorband valley held open by force and subsidies (Ferdinand, 1959:18-19).

[3]On the Hazaras during the time of Shah Rukh, see Price (1821, Vol. III:534-35); of Shah Zaman, see Elphinstone (1815, Vol. II:212); and of Abdul Rahman, see Kakar (1968).

The Hazara territories, then, during this period were essentially beyond the pale of the Afghan groups lying to their south and east.

During the eighteenth and nineteenth centuries a solidifying confederation of Afghan tribes began to press with growing intensity on the southern and eastern flanks of the Hazaras. Raverty wrote:

> Within the last century and a half or two centuries, especially from the time that the Ghalzi Afghans threw off the yoke of the Safawis [under Mir Wais, 1729-32], they began to encroach on the Hazarah people, and to thrust them back towards the west and on account of the steady increase of some branches of the Ghalzis, many of whom are *ilats, kochis,* or nomads, this is still going on. The Durranis, in other parts have been doing the same. . . . (Raverty, 1888:35 approx., quoted in Ferdinand, 1959:12).

The central regions of Afghanistan were gradually feeling the pressure of the growing Afghan confederation which was centralized at first in Kandahar but later in Kabul. Masson wrote of the district of Wardak that prior to the last century it had been

> possessed by the Hazaras, who, about one hundred years since, were expelled by the Afghans. The Hazaras would also seem to have held the country from Karabagh to Ghazni, but have been in like manner partially expelled. Indeed, the encroachments of the Afghan tribes are still in progress (Masson, 1942, Vol. II:224).

It was during this period, that is, early in the nineteenth century, that the region of Bamian was said to have come under the control of the Kabul ruler, Zaman Shah; it was, nonetheless, subject to slave raiding by the peoples of its northern boundaries (Burnes 1834, Vol. II:165; Dollot, 1937:285; Elphinstone, 1815; Vambrey, 1864:213 ff.; Wood, 1841).

Besides being pushed back, as they had been from Wardak, the Hazaras were also gradually being brought under subjection to the Afghan confederation. Burnes reported on the situation during the 1830s as follows:

> The Hazaras of Dihzungee are nearly independent; those of Dih-Koondee altogether so. At Kara Bagh they come down upon the plains beyond Ghuzni and are subject to Cabool, as are those of Jaghoree, Behsud and Fouladee [sic] (1834:230).

The localities to which he refers indicate the geographical range of Afghan control; firm around Ghazni, but farther out less so, until at Deh Kundi there was no control at all.

## Bamian in the Nineteenth Century

At about this time Lieutenant John Wood travelled through Bamian. His report indicates that the control of Bamian had in the recent past fallen alternately to the ruler of Qunduz and the ruler of Kabul. At the time of his journey through Bamian it was subject to the ruler of Qunduz, who collected his tribute in slaves. Kabul's control seemed to reach only as far as Hajigak Pass, the Kalu entrance into the basin (Wood, 1841:198, 200).

Both the rulerships of Qunduz and Kabul were Sunni, the rulership of the Qunduz area being Uzbek and that of Kabul being Afghan. Bamian, in contrast, seemed to be occupied totally by Imami Hazaras, for Wood saw no Tajik (i.e., Sunni) populations in Bamian (1841:206). The Uzbeks, because of their traffic in slaves, were deeply abhorred by the Hazaras of Bamian.

> . . . Generally they speak with detestation of the practice of manstealing, and never mention the Uzbeks, who enslave them, but in terms of loathing and hatred (Ibid., 1841:200).

Even after Bamian eventually came under the firm grip of the Kabul rulers, it was subject to slave raiding attacks from the north. Some elderly persons remember from their childhood stories of those raids. The old fortified buildings (qalaas), constructed to house a number of families, most of which have now crumbled, were made in defense against such raiders, but the development of local defenses and the strengthening of government power in Bamian finally terminated the slave raids during the time of Sher Ali Khan (1863-67, and 1869-79).

During the mid-nineteenth century the Tagaw of Bamian seemed securely held by the ruler of Kabul, Dost Mohammad Khan. Nevertheless a great Hazara coalition controlling the southern and eastern portions of Bamian, as well as most of the Hazarajat (south of Koh-i-Baba) had formed under the leadership of Mir Yazdan Bakhsh of Besud. To the north of Bamian Mir Mohammed Ali Beg, ruler of Sayghan, was still successfully raiding Bamian and other parts of the Hazarajat for slaves whom he gave in tribute or sold to superior powers in Turkestan. To the west of Bamian tribal states existed independent of Kabul or Qunduz control (Ferrier, 1857; Masson, 1842, Vol. II).

The strategic localities along the main caravan routes into the Tagaw of Bamian had to be controlled in order to safeguard the Tagaw. Consequently, as the Tagaw came under a more effective hegemony, the lines of access into and out of Tagaw were also brought under control, usually by treaty and subsidy, sustained by the threat of force. The strongest coalitions on the rim of the basin were those that controlled these passageways through the mountains. Thus Mir Yazdan Bakhsh, who controlled the Hajigak route into Bamian, dominated the southern and eastern rim of the basin. Mir Mohammed Ali Beg, who controlled the Aqrobat route into Bamian, dominated the northern rim of the basin.

Neither of these rulers was directly subservient to the stronger powers located in Kabul and Turkestan, but under pressure they each paid certain forms of tribute: Mir Yazdan Bakhsh of Besud paid to Kabul and Mir Mohammed Ali Beg of Sayghan paid to Qunduz.

## The Marginal Highlands in the Nineteenth Century

The growth of Kabul power brought a firmer political hand into these marginal districts. Sher Ali Khan, in quelling rival attempts for the throne during his first reign (1863-1867), succeeded in pacifying many of the northern regions of Turkestan and thus may have brought a new measure of security and stability to Bamian.

Kakar (1968:209) indicates that the Sheykh Ali Hazaras occupying the eastern fringe of Bamian were first pacified during the reign of Sher Ali Khan. These Hazaras, located on the routes from Ghorband west into Bamian and north into Turkestan, had consistenly taxed or plundered the caravans that travelled through their territory. These "Sheykh Ali Hazaras" may have included the closely related Hazara populations inhabiting Shibar and Kalu, who today call themselves Dargan (Darghu) Hazaras, as well as the true Sheykh Alis who nowadays mainly inhabit the region east and northeast of Shibar. As the Sheykh Alis were later forcibly displaced by Amir Abdul Rahman Khan of Kabul, some of the ties of relationship between these groups may have been forgotten. Kakar (1968: 199) in any case says that "Sheykh Alis" inhabited "both sides of the southwest end of the Hindu Kush," that is, the region here called the southern highlands of east-central Afghanistan.

Sher Ali Khan's second reign (1869-1879) saw the gradual decline of central authority, and after his death the Sheykh Alis resumed their practice of plundering caravans on the Kabul-Turkestan road. Later, Abdul Rahman Khan, who forced his way to the Amirate of Kabul about a year after the death of Sher Ali Khan, sent three successive punitive expenditions against this group early in his reign (1881, 1882, 1883).

One of these raids may have been in retaliation for a specific act of brigandage upon a caravan in which the wife of Amir Abdul Rahman was travelling to Kabul. The year in which this event occurred is obscure, but it is known among these people as "the year of the *lak.*" Two or three hundred Hazara men at some time during Abdul Rahman's reign raided this caravan in the vicinity of Hajigak Pass. They took everything of value but allowed the royal lady and her party to go without further insult. The Amir, however, appears to have been easily able to gain his retribution on these outlaws, for he jailed some of the Hazara leaders, placing a fine of 100,000 afghanis[4] (one lak) on each of them

[4]The afghani is the monetary unit of Afghanistan. Its value today is roughly one and a half cents. At that time it was worth many times more.

payable before their release, while other persons sought by the government fled to the north and stayed away until Habibulah Khan, his son, upon taking the rulership, commuted their sentences. Altogether about ten laks (i.e., 1,000,000) of afghanis were actually paid in fines by those rich enough to obtain the release of these prisoners.

## The Solidification of Politico-Religious Identities

The rulers of Kabul were gradually extending a stronger political presence into central Afghanistan. Kakar's resumé of the tribute payments being made to Abdul Rahman portrays the range of Afghan control in the Hazarajat during the early years of his reign.

> By 1886 all Hazara tribes paid land revenue and taxes on cattle and even marriage fees. But the revenue was not paid in a uniform manner . . . whereas some tribes such as the Behsud . . . Deh Mardad and Sheikh Ali paid 1/4 + 1/10 of their produce of their lands, other tribes such as the Mohmad Khwaja . . . Balkabi . . . Deh Zangi and Deh Kondi . . . paid a fixed amount either on the land or per family. But the rate of revenue on all tribes was increased in various degrees during this period of the Amir's [Abdul Rahman's] reign. The only exception was the Hazaras of Pas-i-Koh (beyond the mountain), who mainly occupied Uruzgan. . . . They were the largest of the tribes, and so far had successfully defied all attempts to obtain their submission (Kakar, 1968:210).

The gain in Afghan control over the Hazara territories that had taken place since the time when Burnes described the range of Afghan government control was the result of a gradual adjustment in the balance of power between Afghans and the Hazaras of central Afghanistan. The Afghan confederation was clearly becoming dominant, and thus was increasingly able to exact tribute from more of the Hazara tribes. As a consequence of this growing Afghan superiority some adjustments were occurring in the frontier zone between the territories of the Hazaras and the Afghans. As each Hazara tribe was brought under the suzerainty of the Afghan rulers, this frontier zone was being pushed farther into the central highlands of the country.

The social boundary between these two groups was changing in another way: they were beginning to formulate their differences as sectarian differences. This change in their identities vis-a-vis each other emerged as the Afghan coalition became a Sunni-dominated State and as the wars of Afghan conquest, which finally led to the complete subjugation of the Hazaras, congealed the support for the State in terms of loyalty to the Sunni faith and the resistance against the State, in the case of Hazara resistance, in terms of loyalty to the Imami faith.

Afghanistan began to take the form of a nation during the reign of Amir

Abdul Rahman. The Amir during his rule attempted, on the one hand, to mold an institution of rulership to replace the confederation of Afghan tribes on which the Amirate was based, and on the other hand, to stretch his military and administrative control across a landscape that had been awarded him by an Anglo-Russian agreement. As the Afghan ruling institution took form, the historic social foundations of authority inherent in the Amir's power were molded into it. One of these foundations lay in the traditional support of Sunni religious leaders. These persons controlled the legal and educational traditions on which the administration of justice was based. Even as early as more than a century before Abdul Rahman, these learned scholars of the Islamic religion had exerted great influence on the Afghan rulership.

> Power over the actions of the monarch was also vested in the Muslim clergy, who were in charge of learning, education, the interpretation of Shari'a law, the administration of justice, and the supervision of public morality through the office of Mohtasib.[5] They enjoyed economic self-sufficiency and wielded great power (Elphinstone, 1815:214-15; see also 527, 540).

The state being formed in Kabul during the time of Abdul Rahman, therefore, leaned heavily upon these authorities of the Islamic faith. That all of them were Sunnis witnessed to the strength of the Sunni persuasion in the regions which politically undergirded the Kabul Amirate. These were the regions surrounding Kabul, Ghazni, and Kandahar and the Afghan-dominated territories mainly to the east and south of these cities.

In addition to the Amir's attempts to form a ruling institution the necessity to subdue the entire territories allotted to Afghanistan also contributed to the forging of Amir Abdul Rahman's government into a Sunni institution. This necessity was pressed upon the Amir by two dangerous uprisings, each of which, by testing his power, forced him to solicit Sunni support.

The first took place in 1888. It was led by Abdul Rahman's own cousin, Ishaq Khan, who had been granted "ownership" of Turkestan by the Kabul Amir. Abdul Rahman's attempt to subjugate Turkestan congealed his support as a self-conscious Sunni coalition, for the Amir attempted to gather support by invoking religious values. He

> directed his efforts to mobilize religious and public opinion against Ishaq. The mullas and elders of Kabul and Jalalabad gave him a *fetwa* [ecclesiastical or judicial edict] to the effect that Ishaq was a rebel . . . they called on all the tribes to act against Ishaq. Further, he gave out that Ishaq's

[5] An attendant of the court empowered to check upon and enforce the observance of religious precepts and duties.

> rebellion was due to Russia and thus they called the suppression of the insurrection "a religious duty" (Kakar, 1968:194).

By suggesting that Ishaq had entered into league with Russia they insinuated that he had compromised his faith for the sake of personal advantage.

In contrast to Abdul Rahman's uniform support by the Sunnis within his realm, Ishaq Khan's following was religiously more diverse. He and the main body of his supporters were Sunnis, but he was also helped by Sheykh Ali Hazaras, who were Imamis.

A few miles south of Khulm (Tashqurghan) the Afghan forces of Abdul Rahman joined in battle with the Uzbek-Sheykh Ali forces of Ishaq Khan. In this conflict Abdul Rahman nearly lost his forces, but owing to the timidity of Ishaq Khan, who fled from the battle, the Amir of Kabul was eventually able to defeat the army of Turkestan. Once in control, the Amir inflicted savage punishments on the most prominent of the insurrectionists. A large number of the Sheykh Alis, for their part in the revolt, were removed en masse from their territory on the eastern and north-eastern flank of Bamian and dispersed throughout Afghanistan.

The second uprising against the Amir of Kabul took place on the heels of the first. After the removal of the Sheykh Alis the Amir appointed a new governor to Bamian and gave him broad powers and a large body of troops. The Amir's objective was to use Bamian as the gateway through which he would accomplish a "peaceful penetration" (Kakar, 1968:210) into the Hazarajat, the mountainous region of central Afghanistan which lay to the west and south (over the Shah-Foladi mountain) of the Bamian basin. As the influence of the Kabul government was being more firmly exerted in the Hazarajat, however, a wholesale Hazara rebellion erupted barely a year after Abdul Rahman's defeat of the Sheykh Alis and the strengthening of his hold on Bamian (Kakar, 1968; Fletcher, 1965:127). Indicative of the control that Kabul exercised over Bamian by this time is the fact that during the Hazara revolt, which at one time involved nearly the whole of the central mountainous regions of the country south and west of Bamian, Bamian itself never openly participated in the revolution (Kakar, 1968: 222-23).

The bloody war that ensued between the Hazaras of Central Afghanistan and the Amir of Kabul was formulated for both sides as a sectarian conflict. Powerful religious coalitions took shape on both sides. The Amir's following became a Sunni coalition more firmly cemented together than ever before.

> Because the Hazaras were Shi'ite [Imami] Muslims and therefore in perpetual enmity with their Sunni neighbors, the Amir obtained *fetwas* from the [Sunni] mullas easily. For the first time, the Khan-e-Mulla of Kabul, in consultation with other mullas, declared religious war against the

> Hazaras. . . . In 600 proclamations which the Amir distributed throughout the country, the Hazaras and all the Shias [Imamis] were declared to be "kafir" [infidel]. The task of inciting the Sunnis was entrusted to the Sunni mullas who, in the religious preaching spared no efforts in condemning the Hazaras to death. . . . To keep up the spirit of war, stipendiary mullas were ordered to accompany the tribal levies, and preach *ghaza* [holy conquest] to them (Kakar, 1968:213).
>
> It was for these reasons that for the first time all the Sunni population rallied to the Amir. It increased his power and prestige, and infused a sense of unity among his subjects (Ibid.: 227).

The Hazaras, on the other hand, were welded together as an Imami coalition in opposition to this Sunni power.

> Never in the past had the Hazaras been so united among themselves as they now were against the Amir. In an assembly . . . Timur Shah a *Sayyed* descendant of Imam Musa Reza, was elected as their Khalifa for the purpose of religious war against the Amir. . . . The Hazaras declared "We will fight for one true God and his prophet, and for Ali against these Kafirs and allies of Kafirs" (Kakar, 1968:218).

The political hub of the Hazara resistance lay in Uruzgan, but at the time of the most widespread Hazara rebellion the Hazaras of Deh Kondi, Deh Zangi, Daya, Folad, Besud, Jaghori, and Gizao were also insurgent (Kakar, 1968:212). In the fall of 1892 the Afghan army pushed into the heart of Hazara territories and effectively quenched all resistance at Uruzgan. But the next spring some of the Hazaras rose again, the first of whom were the Hazaras on the southern side of Koh-i-Baba, where no garrison had been left. This uprising included at least the Hazaras of Besud, Deh Zangi, and Yak Awlang, for the decisive battles were fought against these groups. Whether the Hazaras of the north side of Shah Foladi mountain, the highest ridge of the Koh-i-Baba, joined in the insurrection is not known. But the fact that one of the final engagements took place at Yak Awlang suggests that the western rim of Bamian may have been involved.

By the end of the bloody years of war between the Amir and the Hazaras the Hazarajat was almost desolated. The Amir, as before, relocated his enemies. To replace them, large numbers of Afghans were encouraged to settle in Uruzgan. In addition, the Afghan nomadic tribes who assisted his cause were awarded indisputable grazing rights in central Afghanistan, including the slopes of the massive Koh-i-Baba. The whole of central Afghanistan was finally subdued.

A third conquest by the Amir demonstrated the extent to which the Afghan rulership had acquired a sense of Sunni identity. Amir Abdul Rahman attacked and conquered the pagan peoples of Kafiristan, "Country of Infidels," and renamed that territory Nuristan, "Country of Light." Afterward, he accepted the title *Zia al-Milat-wa-al-Din,* "Light of the Nation and the Religion." In the process of subjugating the diverse and dissident populations of his country, he had consolidated an institution of rulership. He had, moreover, formed it as a coalition of Sunnis, dominated in important respects by the authorities of the Sunni sect.

## Subsequent Highland Resistance

After those battles of the last century, the highland groups of Bamian, though forcibly subdued, in their own way continued to manifest a measure of hostility and insolence toward the Kabul government. In the 1920s during the reign of King Amanullah, the Mir of the Foladi valley, Mosen Beyg, whenever visiting the seat of government in the markaz, was accompanied by a bodyguard of 1,000 horsemen.[6] Indeed, on an occasion when the King himself was visiting the province, the Mir failed to show him appropriate respect; he was consequently jailed, and his family was moved to another district.

The unwillingness of the highland groups to accept the authority of Kabul was evident again during the chaotic period of Bache-Saqaw's reign after he had successfully led a revolt against Amanullah in 1929. After Bache-Saqaw took the rulership of Kabul he was recognized by the populations of Tagaw in Bamian, but the populations in the margins vigorously opposed him. As a result of their opposition, the populations of Tagaw were in danger of being overrun. The Tajiks of the markaz, however, were barely saved by the arrival of troops who had forced their way into the basin from the capital. Their presence at the markaz was clearly sufficient to quell the rebellious Hazaras: prominent Sayyed and Hazara houses in Foladi and Shibar were ransacked and burned and the people fled into the mountains. Some leaders in strategic valleys were executed.

Three informants described incidents in which the populations of Shibar resisted Bache-Saqaw authority. One of these descriptions of resistance was given by a would-be participant in the resistance.

> In the time of Bache-Saqaw the brother of the deposed King Amanullah was travelling in Hazarajat to gather support for him. I had been sent along with several others to join the followers of the former King. We carried money in the form of silver coins sewed in our belts, which made them extremely heavy because at that time 1000 afghanis, pure silver, weighed about 20 pounds. Each of us was carrying 2500 afghanis, that is about 50 pounds apiece, but on the way some Tajiks, whom we at first took to be friendly, robbed us of our horses, money, and firearms. So the result was that we lost everything and were no help to the King. . . . After

[6]This information was given by his grandson.

> Amanullah lost the battle with Saqaw in Kabul, we heard that 600 men from Amanullah's army were coming to Shibar to join our resistance against Saqaw. Only 300 of these reached Shibar, the others having been killed or frightened away. These stood with the people of Shibar for nine months of trouble.

Another of these incidents was told by a person who as a child had seen some of the action.

> When Saqaw became King it was quiet in our district at first. But when we refused to acknowledge him, then trouble began. His soldiers came several times. The first time we were all in our qalaa [fortified dwelling]. The women and children were sent to the mountains. My awdurzada [FaBr], his son, and several other men in my qawm stayed behind. They had only muzzle-loading rifles. The soldiers took my uncle, his son, and five others of my qawmi and killed them. They took away all our things on the backs of our donkeys. They broke down the doors of the houses, and if they found people inside they killed or wounded them. Then they burned our houses. They came at other times. In the end we had nothing left. All of Shibar suffered from Saqaw, but our valley suffered most.

Another description of resistance to Saqaw was told by a relative of the Musa Amin mentioned in this account:

> In the year of Saqaw, there was a caravan train of supplies from Kabul moving to Bamian in logistic support of groups favoring Saqaw in Bamian. As these men came through here we stopped them, captured them, and led them up into Nanqiqol and kept them there. There were 20 or 30 of them. They were taken to the house of Musa Amin where they were hospitably treated, but their goods were taken from them and divided among the people. Then they were kept prisoner for some time until a contingent from Bamian came looking for the lost caravan. The people heard they were coming and many of them fled into the mountains. They at first considered killing their captives, but Musa Amin and Kabir Khan decided to save them. So they agreed to move them up to the mountains at night. That night, along the way, Musa Amin, in a sudden panic, ran away, leaving Kabir Khan alone with the prisoners. So he took them by himself and set them free at the place previously appointed, high in the mountains to the north of Nanqiqol.
>
> Back in Nanqiqol, when the soldiers in pursuit of the missing goods and men reached Nanqiqol, all the people had fled into the mountains, but they were able to catch Musa Amin as he was returning alone from the mountains. They kept him overnight. After discussing what to do with him they decided to kill him by hanging him by his feet and shooting at

> him. Then as Musa Amin was being hung up, one of the men said he would like to have his clothes. They were nice ones, why not take off his clothes first, so they would not be spoiled with blood when he was shot. Then as they were about to take off his clothes, he said to them, "Will you kill a Muslim naked?" Then they conferred among themselves and finally the commanding officer decided to wait overnight. Then during the night some of the released soldiers arrived from the mountains where Kabir Khan had released them and they identified Musa Amin as the man who had cared for them and fed them well during their stay there. So the man was saved from execution.

Nadir Shah Khan, who finally overturned Saqaw, was welcomed as the new King by the Hazaras. In succeeding years, however, as his government grew in strength and established more branches in the mountainous regions, his officials were treated coldly. The *alaqadars* (chief administrators of the government rural stations) assigned to Shibar, for example, were not well received, and until permanent buildings were finally erected for them and their staff, they were obliged to live in inhospitable quarters grudgingly provided by the local elders, and several times they had to shift their locations.

## Contemporary Tension and the Centers of Power

Contemporary political tensions in the east-central region of Afghanistan continue to express, to a milder degree, the historic opposition between lowlander and highlander and between Sunni and Imami. The entire area is now clearly under Afghan suzerainty, but the lowland populations are more fully identified with the developing Afghan nation than are the highland populations. The historic Sunni centers of power in Afghanistan are firmly held by a single administration and serve as the central bases of power from which the Afghan ruling institution exerts its influence on the less accessible and less firmly controlled regions of the country. Four centers of Sunni political influence bear upon the eastern highlands of east-central Afghanistan: Ghorband, Bamian (the markaz), Duab-i-Mezarin, and Doshi. These lowlands, besides being occupied by Sunni populations, are loci of government stations.

The sizable Imami populations in these districts are located mainly in the surrounding highlands. They have been traditionally slow to accept outside authority and have resisted the encroaching Sunni state. Even though their military potential has been decisively quenched, the social distance between them and the Afghans, once established as an Imami-Sunni distinction, has remained. As a result, the continuance of Imami religious practices has enabled the Hazara Sayyed populations of central Afghanistan to remain apart from the national society.

Imami and Ismaili influence, then, is restricted merely to networks of religious clientage. These networks converge on the religious authorities, the Saints of the Imami and Ismaili sects, who provide theological guidance for their clients and collect and redistribute their religious contributions. The authorities to whom the non-Sunni populations of Bamian contribute all reside outside the basin. One Imami authority lives at Yak Awlang to the west. Another is in Kabul to the east. And the third is the Ismaili Saint whose home is near Doshi in the southern Hindu Kush highlands. These authorities and their clients of course are clearly subject to Afghan control, but their importance among the sizable non-Sunni populations of central Afghanistan has endowed them with great influence and, as a consequence, has occasioned the wary surveillance of the Afghan government.

## POLITICAL PROCESSES

### Processes in Bamian History

This review of the political history of Bamian reveals three political patterns that seem to relate to the problem set for this analysis. The first is the contrast between the degree of outside political influence on the populations of Tagaw, and the degree of their influence on the surrounding highland populations. As a consequence of this differential in the outside influence upon the different parts of the basin, the populations of Tagaw and the marginal highlands have experienced different histories. The history of Tagaw has brought it into relatively close association with political groups outside Bamian: though once subject to Turkestan, Tagaw eventually became subservient to the power of Kabul. The highlands surrounding the Tagaw, on the other hand, have experienced less direct influence from external political forces. Even though in the mid-nineteenth century the markaz of Bamian was the locus of a governorship appointed by Kabul, powerful independent Hazara coalitions emerged to the northeast and southeast of Bamian, drawing into their web of influence—though in some cases only partially—the highland regions marginal to the Bamian basin. On the west smaller coalitions remained independent and probably affected political alignments on Bamian's western rim. Furthermore, although late in the last century Tagaw was firmly held by Amir Abdul Rahman, a pair of Hazara coalitions rebelled against him, the Sheykh Ali Hazaras dwelling in the mountains east and north of Tagaw (including, perhaps, those on the eastern edge of the basin), and a coalition of Yak Awlang, Deh Zangi, Deh Kondi, and Besud Hazaras situated in the highlands west and south of the Bamian basin (including perhaps groups from the western and southern margins within the basin). More recently, when Bache-Saqaw took the rulership of Kabul, although the peoples of Tagaw quickly acknowledged his authority, the highland populations surrounding Tagaw revolted. Tagaw, then, has usually been aligned with the external rulerships attempting to control the Bamian basin while the highlands have often been aligned with movements that opposed these external powers. The populations of Tagaw have been more easily subjugated than their highland neighbors.

The second political pattern expressed in the history of Bamian refines the first. This is the different positions from which three centers of power—Kabul, Turkestan and Hazarajat—have exerted influence on the highland populations of Bamian. For while Tagaw has been firmly held by dominant outside political forces, whether situated in Turkestan or Kabul, the populations of the western, and perhaps southern, highlands have often been aligned to the Hazarajat. The peoples of the eastern highlands, in contrast, as they lie in a zone that has often been marginal to all three power centers, have tended to be independent of, or only sporadically controlled by, these powers.

As the power of the Afghan confederacy centering in Kabul grew, it had to subjugate the other two rival centers of power exerting important sway on the Bamian basin. The only one which posed an enduring threat to Kabul was situated in Turkestan where in ancient times Balkh, and more recently Qunduz and Khulm (Tashqurghan), and currently Mazar-i-Sharif, have been the dominant cities. The influence of Turkestan at one time extended to Bamian, even into portions of the Hazarajat south of Bamian, but as Kabul power expanded, the influence of Turkestan in these regions was pushed back. Eventually, as has been shown, Turkestan was securely grasped by Kabul.

The other center of power influencing Bamian was that of the Hazarajat. The Hazaras in this region united into a single political bloc very late, but their locations in the natural mountain fastnesses of central Afghanistan probably contributed to their remaining independent from Kabul than did Turkestan. Within the district of the Hazarajat political coalitions emerged in different places at different times. The area to the west and south of Bamian centering at Besud was one of these localities; this region was the center of the Hazara coalition formed under Mir Yazdan Bakhsh and included, according to Masson (1842, Vol. II), the valley of Kalu and, by means of treaty and alliance, the regions of Shibar and Sheykh Ali. After the collapse of this coalition, this region seems never again to have coalesced in so large a bloc. Rather, the greater centers of political coalescence in the Hazara territories have been further west and south of Besud probably because of the growing pressure which Kabul was able to exert on this more accessible region of the Hazarajat. The other Hazara localities which, in subsequent history, have become centers of Hazara political force have been Uruzgan, Deh Zangi and Yak Awlang. Deh Zangi and Yak Awlang emerged as important political centers in the Hazarajat when they arose in the final Hazara rebellion against Abdul Rahman. That this area seems to still be an important center of Hazara political cohesion is indicated by the importance of Yak Awlang as an Imami religious center today.

The third social pattern revealed in the political history of central Afghanistan is the fusion of religious and political criteria in the development of political groups in Afghanistan. This cementing together of political and religious identities took place, in the Sunni instance, as the Afghan ruling institution developed according to Sunni outlines of administration and jurisprudence, and as a Sunni military force formed in support of the ruling institution for the invasion of the Hazarajat. In the Imami case, this fusion of political and religious identities developed as an Imami coalition formed to resist the Sunni army. The Sunni force was wielded on behalf of an orthodox faith against a heretical faith, Imamism. The Imamis employed force on behalf of their faith against the heretical faith of Sunnism. The defeat of the Imamis by the Sunnis secured the unrivaled supremacy of Sunni Islam in Afghanistan, and established Sunnism as the "orthodox" faith of the nation. Imamism persists, but by the tolerance of the Sunnis. What has been written about heterodoxy and orthodoxy in another muslim setting could be said about Afghanistan:

> conformity to it [the official credo of the state], however perfunctory, was the token and pledge of loyalty. Orthodoxy meant the acceptance of the existing order, heresy or apostasy its criticism and rejection (Lewis, 1953:62; see also Lambton, 1956).

To be Sunni in Afghanistan is to be in some sense identified with the ruling institution and with the Sunni sources of authority on which its administrative system partially depends. To be Imami is to be identified with the resistance that once warred against, and even now continues in some degree to be isolated from, that ruling institution.

## Ismailism and Political Processes

These patterns suggest two arguments for why Ismailism has developed in the highlands of east-central Afghanistan. The first argument is that these highlands, lying in a zone that has been more or less marginal to all three political centers of gravity, have been relatively free to develop independent or ephemeral political coalitions. For some time neither the political groups dominating Turkestan nor those of Hazarajat have been able to effectively impose themselves on the eastern highlands of east-central Afghanistan, including Shibar. Indeed, even the expanding rulership of Kabul has had difficulty in holding this area within its secure domains. Historically this area has remained at the frontiers of the influences emanating from all three centers of power, and until the ruling institution of Kabul was able to establish secure administrative posts in the rural areas, these groups remained independent of, even recalcitrant toward, outside control. A resistance movement, in which a dissenting group was able to successfully identify itself as independent of these influences, was actually only feasible for groups situated out of range of both Imami and Sunni centers of influence. Ismailism, therefore, developed where the influence of both groups was weak. It could not develop as a form of dissent from Imamism in the western portions of Bamian because the geographical heart of the Imami sect, and thus of Imami political influence, lay just west of the basin; though more inaccessible to Sunni influences than the eastern highlands, this area was more firmly bound into the orbit of the Imami resistance. Only the eastern highlands, therefore, were free enough to form a political movement out of reach from both centers of political influence.

The second argument, already traceable in the foregoing, is set forth here merely as a hypothesis in the absence of verifiable historical information on the actual emergence of Ismailism in this area. This argument is that Ismailism developed as the populations of the southern Hindu Kush highlands became aware that their interests were different from those of the Imamis and Sunnis whose centers of influence lay far outside their own territories; accordingly, they began to express their independence and recalcitrance toward these outside groups in terms of a dogmatic formulation emphasizing their discreteness from the other two politically significant groups imposing on the area.

In central Afghanistan the Imami sect, rather than being the subjugated minority that it is in Bamian Tagaw and in most of Afghanistan, has been the politically dominant sect. Resistance to the Imami-dominated society in Hazarajat, therefore, may have been expressed through the conscious espousal of a distinctly contrary religious doctrine. Inasmuch as the identifying criterion of allegiance to the State was allegiance to Sunnism and the criterion of resistance against the State was Imami allegiance, the criterion of membership in an independent movement became formulated as loyalty to a sect clearly different from both Sunnism and Imamism.

It is not necessary to attribute an anthropomorphic consciousness of this social process to the societies that became Ismailis. Rather, it seems sufficient to say that these groups grew aware that their political interests were different from those of the Imami coalitions of the Hazarajat as well as those of the Sunni powers in Kabul and Turkestan, and accordingly, coalesced in a movement of independence from them; moreover, since the identities of these external powers were characteristically couched in religious terms, it was natural that the coalescence of these marginal populations in opposition to external pressures should be under the leadership of personages having the theological sophistication to formulate their contrary orientation in theological terms. A third sect seems to have been the appropriate alternative in view of the social conditions. The ritual practices and secret beliefs of the Ismailis, then—like the wearing of the veil and the *checia* in pre-independence Algeria—became for these people part of their "language of refusal" (Bourdieu, 1962:157), setting them apart from the alien powers and cultures who had imposed themselves upon them.

The third sect, Ismailism, is considered more heretical than Imamism, and as such its ideological "distance" corresponds to the spatial isolation of its adherents. Ismailism, a greater heresy than either Sunnism or Imamism, appeared in the frontier zone beyond the reach of both.

The previous isolation of the marginal highlands from State control has in recent years diminished as modern methods of transport and communication have been introduced. All the populations of the basin are feeling its influence more keenly. It seems unlikely, therefore, that Ismailism will grow any further. Both Ismailism and Imamism are likely to decline in size and influence as the Afghan government's influence expands in the Imami- and Ismaili-controlled regions of the country. The processes of local fissioning described in this study will probably never be active again.

# VII

# CONCLUSION

## SUMMARY OF THE ARGUMENT

THE first chapter posed some questions about the mosaic of religious groups in Bamian and the succeeding chapters developed a series of arguments which, taken together, appear to answer them.

First, *why are the religious sects of Bamian distributed in a regular way?* The answer seems to lie in economic and political influences emanating from outside Bamian. Due to Tagaw's easily controlled agricultural wealth and its strategic position at the heart of the basin where trade lines converge, its populations have been more strongly influenced by the Sunni-dominated trade network of the nation than the highland populations. As national trade grew with the improvement of transportation and communication Tagaw's wealth became increasingly absorbed into the national trade system, and its populations became oriented toward a cash economy, and toward Sunnism. It is not known, however, how the formerly Imami populations of Tagaw were actually succeeded by Sunnis. Perhaps they converted to Sunnism to gain better opportunities in the national market, or perhaps they were pushed out of the heartland by Sunnis who immigrated to take advantage of attractive opportunities in Tagaw. In any case, the transformation that took place in Tagaw did not occur in the surrounding highlands where the populations are less accessible to foreign economic influences and where agricultural production is more modest. Consequently, the highland populations, existing primarily by subsistence activities, are only marginally integrated into the national economy. And they are not Sunnis, but Imamis and Ismailis.

The political influences from outside Bamian have also affected social alignments in the basin. The populations of Bamian have socially differentiated primarily in terms of their relation to the Sunni ruling institution and the opposing Imami religious sect. The populations on Tagaw are those most accessible to Sunni influence and have identified with Sunnism, while most of those in the highlands have expressed their differences with the Sunni institution by identifying with Imamism. Among those living in Shibar and Kalu, however, some have refused to identify with either Sunnism or Imamism, and have become Ismailis.

The Ismailis dwell in a frontier zone where the influences of external power groups have historically been weak. In terms of larger political influences, they are distributed in an area marginal to three political centers—Kabul, Afghan Turkestan, and Hazarajat. In terms of a smaller range of political influences, the sect lies between the Sunni-controlled lowlands of Bamian and Ghorband, and between two centers of Imami influence, Kabul and Yak Awlang. In this historically inaccessible and intransigent area the third bloc has congealed, loyal to a religious authority dwelling in its own highland territories. Ismailism therefore can be regarded as a kind of frontier polity which, to express its independence and interests both from Sunnism and Imamism, has formulated its social distinctiveness as a different religious sect.

*Why are factional differences expressed in religious terms?* The reason for this is implied above. Political blocs within the basin have formulated their distinct identities in terms of their relationship to each other and in terms of the categories with which the power centers have become identified. The divisions within the communities of Shibar are formulated in religious terms because sectarian categories are the overriding social distinctions in the society and because the ecological setting in Shibar is more favorable to internal division.

*Why do communities in Shibar divide while those elsewhere in Bamian do not?* Fission among community members actually does take place throughout Bamian, but only in Shibar do ecologic circumstances allow those losing a dispute to remain on their lands. Inherent in Bamian's communities everywhere contradictory tensions act both to pull its members together and to rend them apart. Dissenting persons in these communities generally either must acquiesce to community opinion or leave home, and their emigration enables their communities to retain the appearance of social solidarity.

The strength of this kind of solidarity, however, varies according to the different ecologic circumstances of each community. Ecologic conditions in Shibar are most conducive to a breakdown in community solidarity because of the importance of rainfall agriculture, which unlike irrigation agriculture, requires little group solidarity. Nevertheless, even in Shibar a community does not allow dissident persons to remain on their lands unless they are situated where the natural water supply is abundant and accessible. Division can take this form in such communities where factioning without spatial relocation is a feasible option.

*How does conversion take place if it is said to be impossible?* Conversion of individual families and small groups takes place under the circumstances described above, and represents an attempt on the part of disputing persons to realign themselves to another group of sharing kinsmen. Such a social realignment for tactical reasons eventually becomes expressed in ideological terms so that the disputants become reckoned as kinsmen of the new group and their former kinship ties are discarded.

## SOME GENERAL APPLICATIONS

This solution seems applicable to two problems of ethnic and religious grouping elsewhere in Afghanistan. One of these is the lack of congruence between ethnic and religious identities in Afghanistan. Generally the ethnic and religious criteria of social identity coincide so that a Hazara is assumed to be Imami, a Tajik to be Sunni, etc. This coincidence is not perfect, however. While most Afghans are Sunnis, there are also Imami Afghans and Ismaili Afghans.[1] Whereas most Hazaras are Imamis or Ismailis, there are Sunni Hazaras as well—the Deh Zainat Hazaras of Badgis (northwest of Mazar-i-Sharif) and their relatives, the Tatars.[2] And people known as "Tajiks," the second largest ethnic category in the country, are not all Sunnis: in eastern and northern Afghanistan and elsewhere in Central Asia Tajiks are Sunnis; but in western Afghanistan (e.g., Ghorian) and Iran they are Imamis, and in the Pamir Mountains "Tajik" groups (called "Mountain Tajiks" or "Pamir Tajiks") are Ismailis (Fig. 11).

A complete explanation of this irregularity is impossible now, but it is interesting to note that the territorial locations of these various kinds of groups suggest that ethnic and religious alignments in Afghanistan as a whole approximate the pattern we have delineated for Bamian. The several kinds of Sunni populations control the economic centers of Afghanistan; the different kinds of Imamis occupy marginal lands, either mountainous regions (as in Hazarajat) or desert lands (as in western Afghanistan, e.g., Ghorian); and the different kinds of Ismailis occupy the most remote lands of the Hindu Kush-Pamir mountain range between the centers of Sunni and Imami influence. Such a distribution is due partly to the nature of the varied landscape itself, which provides shelter to the different interest groups, and partly to the sectarian nature of the Afghan state.

The other problem to which our analysis may apply is the relation between race and cultural identity in Afghanistan. Many ethnic groups are believed to be racially distinct and therefore easily distinguishable by phenotype as well as culture. In Bamian, racial type, while grossly related to ethnic identity, is not a precise criterion. The Hazaras, though generally Mongoloid, are not all phenotypically distinct and some persons calling themselves "Tajiks" look very Mongoloid. The relations therefore between racial type and cultural identity are rather loose. Some persons, despite their racial appearance, have passed from

[1] The Afghan Ismailis apparently keep their faith very secret, for I know of no one outside the sect who is aware of their existence. I am told that they are a wealthy community of Pushtu-speaking occupational specialists in eastern Afghanistan. They should not be confused with the Roshanis of several centuries ago (Caroe, 1958).

[2] In Ferrier's day (1830s) the Tatars were known as "Tatar Hazaras" or "Hazara Tatars." The Tatars I encountered often identified themselves as initially as Tajik, but eventually explained that they were Tatars. None of them, however, identified themselves as Hazara of any type. The Tatars generally have strong Mongoloid features, like the Hazaras.

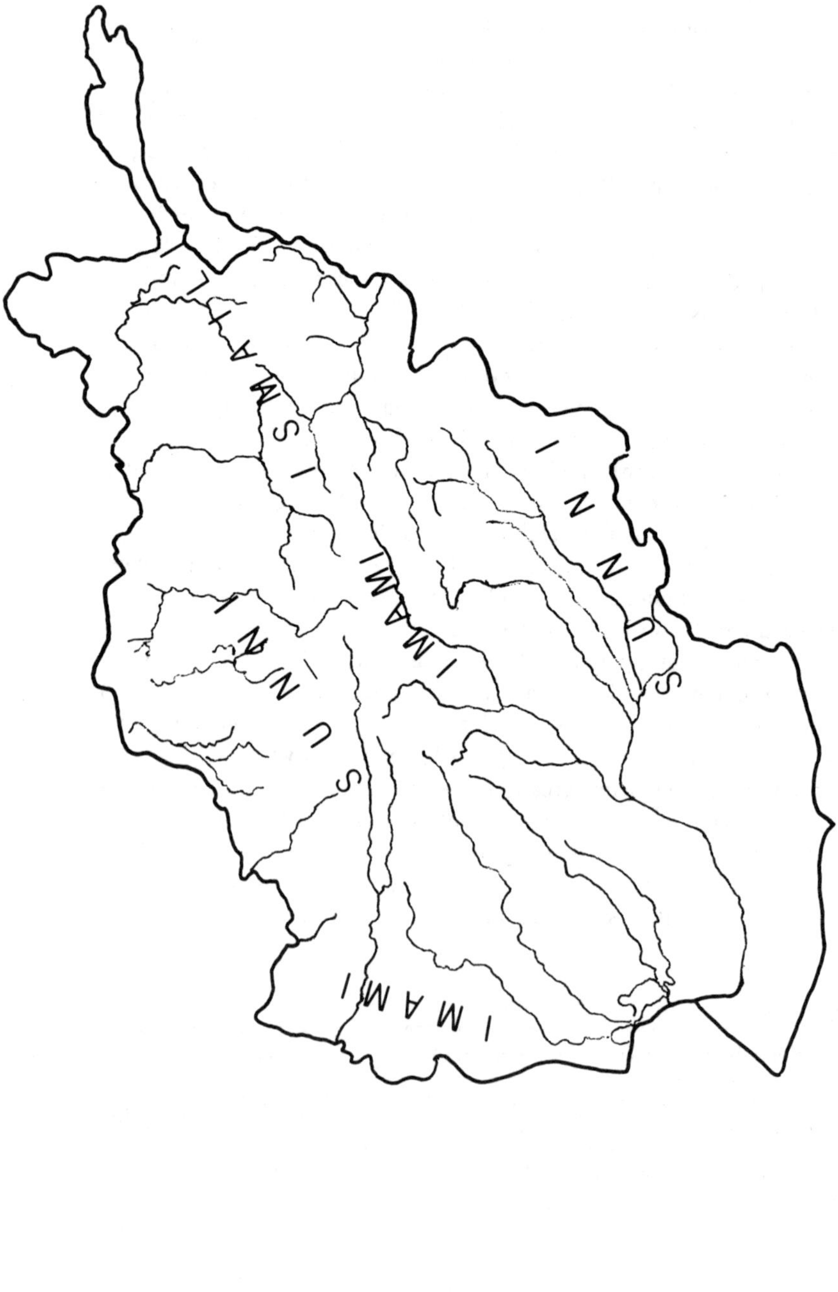


Figure 11. The general location of sects in Afghanistan.

one cultural group to another. As one Hazara said of a sibling of an ancestor, "Dahla became Tajik" (see Bacon, 1958:6, 7, 18). Presumably, a Hazara "becomes Tajik" by identifying with Sunnism and becoming absorbed into the Sunni Tajik population.

The phenotype of an individual would seem to deter such passing if he strongly evinced characteristic racial features and if the society tolerated no intermarriage between racial groups. In Afghanistan Sunni men sometimes marry non-Sunni women, but Hazara men rarely marry Sunni women. Hazara men may in rare circumstances convert to Sunnism and marry Sunni women. Presumably, in such cases the racial identity of these men eventually becomes lost. If not clearly Mongoloid in appearance, the (former) Hazara may himself eventually be regarded as a Caucasian as well as Sunni. If not he, then his children would more certainly be recognized as full members of the Sunni society; they would be more easily considered Caucasian and Sunni, for they would betray fewer distinctive racial features and be fully socialized into Sunni culture.

Not only have individual Hazaras become Tajiks but even whole groups of Hazaras in some areas may have made this transition. The Tatars of Turkestan were once known as Hazara Tatars (Ferrier, 1857) and bear strong Mongoloid features, but today they call themselves "Tajiks" and are Sunnis. Also, there are populations calling themselves "Tajiks" in Jalmesh and Ghandak whose appearance and kinship terms suggest a Mongol ancestry; unlike most Tajiks they terminologically distinguish between elder and younger siblings, a trait commonly found among Hazaras and Mongols (Bacon, 1958).

## THEORETICAL CONCLUSIONS

Implicit in the argument of this study has been a broad claim: that the ethnic and sectarian groups forming the rural mosaics of the Middle East and Central Asia, and specifically of Afghanistan, are not merely different cultural groups transmitting their characteristic traditions from the past, but are also political units existing in tension within their socio-political contexts.

Such political units have been identified by various terms. Easton (1959) has distinguished rural and minority interest groups in a plural society from national political systems, calling them "parapolitical structures." This distinction is merely one of relative power (see Bailey, 1968). Similarly, Barth (1969*a*) and Abner Cohen (1969) have employed the term "ethnic group" and suggest that ethnicity is merely a form of political grouping:

> Ethnicity is . . . basically a political and not a cultural phenomenon, and it operates within contemporary political contexts and is not an archaic survival arrangement carried over into the present by conservative people (A. Cohen, 1969:178).

Both Barth and Cohen believe that ethnicity may be distinguishable by different kinds of cultural criteria, e.g., race, tribe, caste, language, etc. Therefore the more general term "interest group" is preferred.

Interest groups have two features vital to their existence. First, they share some common economic and political interests and consequently stand together in opposition to other groups and the state. In urban contexts well-to-do interest groups maintain their identities to protect vital economic monopolies (A. Cohen, 1969), while underprivileged groups coalesce to guard what common economic and political interests they share (Morse, 1965; Gonzales, 1970). Similarly, in rural settings minority groups congeal to protect mutual concerns, especially to avoid the increased costs, such as taxation and conscription, of articulating with the national structures.

The second vital feature of interest groups is their cultural distinctiveness. Minority interest groups typically congeal around ethnic and religious customs that characterize their distinctive identity. They are therefore relatively difficult for a ruling institution to control. Abner Cohen (1969:3) has pointed out that ethnic and religious interest groups are especially suitable for evading governmental pressures, for a state can only at great cost control the customs of marriage, kinship, friendship, and ritual among its citizenry. And it is just such customs that can become the social forms around which informal political interest groups congeal.

There is characteristically a tension between an interest group and other similar groups in its field of social relations, but the most decisive tension is that between the group and the state. Bailey has pointed out that interest groups

> are partly regulated by, and partly independent of, larger encapsulating political structures; and . . . so to speak, fight battles with these larger structures in a war which for them seldom, if ever, ends in victory, rarely in dramatic defeat, but usually in a long drawn stalemate and defeat by attrition (1968:281).

The nature of the ruling institution affects interest groups in three ways. First, it influences the degree to which they may remain discrete, solidary units. Abner Cohen has noted that in some African nations tribesmen who immigrate to the cities become less committed to tribal loyalties while in some other countries they become more tribalized. The difference, he suggests, is a consequence of the different poses which the African states take toward their minority groups.

> The degree to which interest groups can develop in a society depends on the type of state system that prevails in that society. Some states permit a high degree of political "pluralism," by allowing the formation of a wide variety of formally organized interest groups. Other states are less

> tolerant . . . , but do not prevent the formation of *informal* interest groups. Yet other states do not tolerate even such informal interest groups and do their utmost to suppress them (A. Cohen, 1969:3).

Second, a state's structures affect the cultural identities of interest groups. Since an interest group, in order to remain apart, must identify itself in distinctly contrastive cultural terms, its cultural identity often appears as a kind of complementary opposite to the identity of the state. Thus, the cultural categories around which a state coalesces defines the terms in which the interest group will express its distinctiveness. As cultural identities of the wider society change, the distinctive cultural features of an interest group may have to adjust also. Abner Cohen (1969) has described how the Hausa of Sabo, Ibadan, reformulated their distinctive characteristics in order to maintain their social identity. In a somewhat different way the categories of social identity in Afghanistan have changed. At one time the identities of political groups were defined in terms of patrilineal descent groups: Hazaras versus Afghans versus Tajiks versus Uzbeks, etc. But as the coalition of Afghan tribes grew into a ruling institution, the disposition of the rulership toward Sunnism—expressed in its application of Sunni (i.e., Hanafi) interpretations of Islamic law in the courts and its appeal for popular support as a Sunni coalition—endowed it with a Sunni identity, though it was still dominated by Afghans. Opposition to the rising Sunni power was expressed in the antithetical sectarian categories of Imamism and Ismailism. Thus, superimposed upon patrilineal descent loyalties there were sectarian loyalties: Sunnis versus Imamis versus Ismailis.

The third way in which state structures affect interest groups is in the location of rural interest group territories. Since the administration and control of interest groups entail costs as well as benefits to the ruling institution, cost-benefit factors set functional limits on the state's ability profitably to control these groups. In rural areas these limits appear as the territorial boundaries forming the interest group mosaic. Thus, the mosaic of rural interest groups traces certain social frontiers of the national administration (see Gellner, 1970).

Such has been the conception of interest group structures employed in this analysis. The interest groups of Afghanistan are not merely traditionalistic, conservative groups which, owing to geographic isolation, have been bypassed by the progress of history in the larger society. They are also political and economic groups whose traditional customs and religious identities help protect vital concerns.

# APPENDIX I

# PUBLIC CEREMONIES

THIS Appendix is a supplement to Chapter IV. The public ceremonies for which kinsmen come together are described in two sections, Rites of Passage and Special Religious Occasions.

## RITES OF PASSAGE

### Childhood Rites

Infant mortality being quite high, the birth of a child is not celebrated elaborately. But if the child lives, the celebrations of his development as a social person successively grow in importance, culminating in the celebration of his marriage, for this is the symbol of his adulthood.

The women are the main persons to celebrate the birth and growth of a child prior to his circumcision. Before he is born, a few women closely related to the pregnant mother join her on a day called *kaalaa-buraani,* "clothes cutting," in order to prepare clothing for the infant. Fruit and rice and meat (*palaw*) is usually served by the more well-to-do families; otherwise bread, pastry, and tea.

Similarly, at the time of the appearance of a baby's first tooth a few closely related persons in wealthy families, mostly women, may eat a meal together called *dandaani* (*dandaan* = "tooth"). *Sarkali,* "headshaving," is done when a boy is one year old. One of the most elderly relatives of the child will shave the child's head in the presence of the close relatives in expression of the hope that the child will grow to the age of the man performing the act. A meal is provided for those who come. The female guests give petty amounts of money (5 to 25 afghanis) as gifts to women of the household. This is called *shakerreyz*, "sugar-pouring."

Circumcision is prescribed for all males of an Islamic community and initiates young men into the body of adult believers who pray together; until circumcised, children of Imami parents, considered unbelievers (*kaafar*), are not allowed to eat from the same dish as the men. In all the sects, boys are circumcised between the ages of three and nine, usually about five.

Circumcision is done in the fall of the year (early Mizan) by an itinerate group of two or three barbers from outside the community, usually Maydaan. They play music on the night before the circumcision. Usually feasts are served that night by the families circumcising a boy. Families who can afford it often spend much on such feasts and invite relatives from far and near to enjoy it with them. Those who cannot afford a feast consisting of rice and meat (palaw) will serve tea and pastry. Next day, before the barbers leave, all the designated boys in the community are circumcised at one time.

## Marriage

Marriage initiates young persons into adulthood. It is considered a religious duty because the Prophet Muhammad married, and his life is considered a standard of faith and practice. To marry, many believe, is to gain merit with God. Not to marry is a sin.

Marriage ceremonies involve more relatives than any other rite of passage and epitomize the intricacy of reciprocal giving between kinsmen. A marriage is joined by a series of increasingly larger social gatherings through which the relatives of the bride and groom endorse the marriage by their presence and their witnessing of the presentations of goods, and express solidarity in the common consumption of food. The consensus of the relatives is the ultimate sanction of the marriage. Even though official registration is necessary, the government is nevertheless dependent on the testimonials of local elders for marriage registration.

The stages of progressive publicity and economic expenditure are the early search for a wife, the proposal, the engagement, the wedding, and the postmarital transactions. These stages are here described in detail because of the importance of the social bonds created by marriage.

When the men get together they talk among other things about girls: who is the new prospect for marriage, how much her bride price may be, who may bid for her, how old she is, whether her parents are ready to marry her off now, etc. They always ask whether she is pretty. Girls in rural communities, being unveiled, may easily be seen, though seldom does a man talk to a girl not closely related. Older men do not marry women they have not first seen. Older as well as younger men can take an interest in young girls because under Islamic law they may have four wives; even more are sometimes had by the very rich in certain remote districts.

The women know better who the prospective brides are and how suitable they may be as wives. While a girl's beauty is important to the men, her temperament is important to the women. Girls known for a bad temper and the daughters of ill-tempered women are not desired.

Arrangements for a first marriage are always made by parents or guardians.

Other marriages are initiated by the adult men themselves. In both cases, however, initial contact is made through representatives (*wakils*), who at first are usually women. A woman on behalf of her son, or (in the mother's absence) her younger brother, approaches the female relatives of the bride and proposes a marriage. Usually first proposals are refused or delayed, so it is expected that several visits will have to be made. Refusals and delays give the girl's family time to inquire about the suitor and to develop a consensus about the proposal. If the girl's family agrees, a male from the boy's family is sent to propose more formally to the girl's father or guardian.

Engagements are commonly made even when the children are quite young. A certain woman, for example, told me that her daughter was engaged to a boy named Mir Amad. He asked for her when she was very young, about five or six years old. He is now 25 and she 14. When he first asked for her the mother and father would not agree. But so many of his family visited them so often, always staying late, that they wore her family out. They finally agreed to give her to Mir Amad, but only later. They, the mother said, would wait another two years, but Mir Amad told me separately that he hoped to marry the next summer.

After the initial proposal is privately accepted a few men from the boy's close relatives–e.g., Fa, Br, FaBr, FaBrSo–bring lump sugar to the girl's family. Everyone eats lump sugar and drinks tea supplied by the girl's family. This is known as "the breaking of hard sugar" (*qand shekestaani*) and signals a private agreement of the marriage.

A few days later at a time set by the girl's father, they come again for a *shirini khori,* "eating sweets," which is the formal engagement ceremony. Tajiks bring only fruit and lump sugar; Hazaras send in advance the necessary ingredients for a feast.[1] If the food served is only fruit and lump sugar it is distributed among the guests by the father of the girl, sometimes in teacups, but sometimes (among the wealthier Tajiks) in small scarves which are then kept as favors by the guests. To the shirini khori more men from the boy's family come, sometimes as many as 50, for richer families, but usually only five or six among the poor. Relatively fewer relatives of the girl attend this feast.

The groom is among the guests. If a meal is served, after the meal the host tells the groom that it was cooked by a certain daughter of his. This indicates his acceptance of the marriage. Commonly, one of the boy's family forthrightly asks the girl's father three times if he has promised his daughter to this boy; each time of course he replies affirmatively. Then they eat the lump sugar and tea together in celebration of this engagement. Finally, they pray that God will bless this agreement. After the shirini khori the boy is allowed to visit his father-in-law but cannot stay overnight.

[1] An example of the goods and amounts sent in advance for a typical shirini khori is the following: two sets of clothes, two or three rings, a pair of shoes, a watch; eight pounds of hard candy, one sheep, sixteen pounds of ghi; eighty pounds of rice.

The women also meet for shirini khori. Prior to the shirini khori some of the close female relatives in the groom's family bring a small gift to the mother of the girl, usually clothing, but sometimes money (perhaps 20 afghanis apiece). Later they bring clothing for the bride, consisting, for example, of gold earrings, a gold ring, a necklace, an embroidered blouse and pantaloons, and a head scarf. In addition to these things, the closest female relatives of the boy–his mother, sisters, and aunts–will each send similar personal items of clothing to the bride. All these gifts are brought to the girl's house on a tray covered with a cloth, and on the way they sometimes sing and play the tambourine. The tray of gifts is paraded on someone's head. At the girl's house, where the women of the bride's family have gathered, the groom's mother gives each item on the tray to the bride's mother, displaying it to everyone present.

The mother of the girl should later reciprocate the specific personal gifts of the groom's female relatives, and if possible, double the amount. The shirini khori among the women mainly consists of giving these gifts and consuming tea and hard sugar. At the very end, the bride sometimes gives her mother-in-law some lump sugar in an embroidered cloth for the groom.

Seldom does a marriage take place earlier than three months after an engagement, and usually it is much later. There are two reasons. One is that engagements are often made years before the girl, and often the boy, reach marriageable age. Another is that the boy's family needs time to muster the funds for the wedding costs and the bride price. In any case, the object of the early engagement ceremonies is to confirm publicly the verbal marriage agreement and to secure it until the marriage can be consummated.

Among the Hazaras agreement on the bride price usually occurs when the proposal is accepted. Customarily, the girl's father asks for an exorbitant amount and then eventually, if seriously interested in engaging his daughter to the suitor, comes down to a price current at the time.

Sometimes, when the marriage cannot be consummated for some months or years the Hazaras hold a *toykhord*, "little marriage," feast. This is essentially similar to the shirini khori but involves more people. The crucial object of toykhord is to make the engagement more public, and hence more secure, by a rather larger feast preliminary to an expected lengthy delay in the actual marriage ceremony. During this period of waiting the boy should take gifts of clothing to his fiancee and to her mother on special occasions, such as on Id or New Year's Day. In return, he is sometimes given a kind of pastry (*qadmal*). He is allowed to sleep in his father-in-law's house without conjugal rights.

When the boy's family is ready for the marriage, several men from the family call on the girl's father and indicate their readiness to have the marriage feast. Among the Tajiks this is the time for finalizing the bride price. As mentioned earlier, among the Hazaras the bride price has usually already been set.

A day for paying the bride price is set. Usually a meal is eaten by a number of males from the two families, the food for it provided by the groom's family. This amount is perhaps around 80 pounds of rice, some firewood, meat, potatoes, ghi, etc. After the meal the bride price is counted out in front of everyone and given to the girl's father.

The amounts of the bride price vary in different areas. Tajiks on the markaz generally pay 10,000 afghanis cash plus the following goods consumed in the wedding feast: 1000 pounds of rice, 150 pounds of ghi, eight lambs or kids, 10 donkey-loads of wood, four loads of brush fuel, 150 pounds of wheat, eight pounds of kerosene, 30 pounds of salt, four pounds of tea, 35 pounds of sugar, 150 pounds of potatoes, 30 pounds of onions.[2] Usually these amounts are quoted in their cash value, as say, 10,000 afghanis for bride price and 3000 afghanis for the feast. Formerly, cash being scarce, most of the bride price was paid in goods. As an example, 20 years ago in the highlands a relatively wealthy man paid the following as bride price: three bulls, three large copper cooking pots, one muzzle-loading rifle and 3000 afghanis in silver coin.

Soon after the payment of the bride price a few of the groom's closest female relatives gather to eat a meal (usually) and pudding (always). Then as a group they take the wedding dress and ornaments for the bride to her house. They don't stay long except to have tea.

*Shaw-i-khina,* "the night of henna," takes place soon afterwards on the night before the wedding. On shaw-i-khina all the members, of the groom's qawm community gather at his house for a feast and put henna on his hands. If it is an intra-qawm community marriage the only members of the qawm community not likely to come are those most closely related to the bride. Her relatives gather at the same time in her house for a similar purpose and the food for this meal, as well as at the groom's house, is provided by the groom's family.

At the groom's house the relatives throw petty amounts of cash for him into a scarf carried by one of his friends. Closer friends are supposed to give more than others. As the gifts are thrown the person carrying the scarf calls out loudly twice the amount each person gave, praising him with the expression, *khanesh aabaad!,* "Long live his house!" This is done among both the women and the men.

The wedding takes place the next day. Sometime before the afternoon ceremony it is customary among the Imamis (and also among many Sunnis, despite the teaching to the contrary by Sunni authorities) for the groom and a few male friends to pay a visit to a nearby shrine. This is to protect him from any secret sorcerous attempts to render him impotent.

In the later afternoon the groom and his male relatives go to the house of the bride—singing, dancing, and shooting a gun, if available—where a large feast

[2] These specific figures are taken from the costs of a wedding that took place about two years ago. The family was not wealthy.

has been prepared from ingredients sent in advance by the groom's family. The mullah-imam of the community performs the marriage ceremony (*neka*). In a recorded ceremony in Shibar the mullah-imam began the ceremony with the following words:

> You who are endowed with purity and greatness, who are in charge of this meeting, you are here with these honorable and respectable people to be witnesses of this event. We want to do this according to the law of Muhammad so that no one will have any complaint. [Then he asked three times if anyone had anything to say against the marriage.]

The neka ceremony concludes with the singing of official papers by the mullah-imam and the mir. Later the judge signs also.

After the neka the groom goes to the room where his bride is waiting with the other women. The groom's path is obstructed by a woman from the bride's family demanding a gift, called *nazr-i-bibi,* "vow or offering to Bibi" (i.e., to Fatema, the daughter of Muhammad). This is supposed to contribute to Fatema's merit in heaven and thus in return win her intercessory favor on their behalf. As the groom enters the room where the bride and other women are waiting, the bride's mother throws coins on him; this is her own money. He in return throws coins on his bride. The female guests pick up most of the money.

The groom and bride are escorted to their relatives, often singing, dancing, and shooting a gun, if available, to the groom's house. They go on foot if the groom's residence is in the same village or neighborhood, or, if further away, on horseback, by car, or truck. A woman from each family accompanies the couple to their home. The one from the bride's family remains over night to obtain the evidence of her virginity, which she carries back to the girl's family. When the wedding party reaches the groom's house the female members of his family throw coins (among the Tajiks) or pastry (among the Hazaras) on the couple. These are gathered up by other persons in the party.

After the girl is deposited in the house, the groom returns outside where his qawmi say a prayer (duwas) for him, that God will bless him and his household. In return he thanks his qawmi for their help. "You have gone to much trouble for my marriage," he tells them, and he concludes with a prayer, such as "May God give wives to those of you who have none and may He reward any supplication you make before Him."

Next day the women of the bride's family come to the groom's house for lunch with the women of his family. They bring the trousseau of the bride at this time.[3] The boy's mother gives a gift known as *khela'at* to seven of the

[3]The items in one Tajik girl's trousseau were as follows: Three boxes of clothing, a mattress and pillow, blankets, a couple of *destarkhans* (cloths on which food is spread), a few handkerchiefs, a *chadari* (veil falling to the ankles), 20 dresses, 20 scarves, 20 pantaloons, four pairs of shoes, 30 hats, (all made by the bride herself), 30 embroidered drop cloths, 30

women closest to the bride, consisting of a scarf and a dress for each. That morning the women are allowed to see the bride but for this privilege they must pay a few coins to the woman who came with her for the night.

The fifth day after the wedding is the day of *takhtakani*, "hitting the board." This is the day when the bride begins to work in the household. The seven women to whom the groom's mother gave gifts supply most of the food for a feast to which the women of the girl's qawm come for a lunch. After this the bride goes to work.

A few days later the groom's mother distributes some of the smaller items (mainly the mirrors and hats) from the bride's trousseau to the women of the household.

A month or so after the wedding, the bride's mother invites her and her husband to come stay for a few days. This is called *paywazi*. They are accompanied on the first night by several men and women from the boy's family. If they live near enough, until the time of paywazi the bride's mother has daily sent a bowl of pudding to the newlyweds. At the paywazi the bride's father, if able, gives her an animal such as a cow, calf, or sheep as a personal gift.

## Death

When a person becomes so sick that it is feared he will die, the relatives gather. The host feeds the visitors and provides them with bedding. The visitors and members of the family do what they can to make the sufferer physically comfortable, but they are equally concerned to support him spiritually. It is believed that the pain of death, though very great (more painful for the sinful man than the righteous), can be relieved by the recitation of the so-called Yasin Sura (XXXIV), which is in the exact middle of the Quran. A relative repeats the Yasin Sura for the afflicted one through his final moments of death. It is also believed absolutely necessary that he remember the muslim creed in order to identify himself as a true believer to the angels who are to examine his beliefs soon after his death; consequently, a relative continually repeats the creed to him. Further, as it is believed that immediately upon his death Satan will tempt him by offering him wine (which is forbidden to muslims) to quench his thirst, a relative will sprinkle droplets of water on his lips to assuage his thirst and thus help him to resist. The phrase "water is dropping on his lips" (*labesh ab chakak mekona*) is a euphemism for "he is dying."

draw-strings for her pantaloons, 30 mirrors, 30 combs, two pounds of thread, a box of cosmetics, one rather simple silver necklace and one expensive (valued at 500 afghanis) necklace, a pair of silver bracelets, and a pair of upper arm bands in which amulets are carried, 20 rings, a coat (*chapan*) for the groom, and turbans for his closest friends who took part in the marriage ceremony.

Immediately after death the hands are laid across the body and the legs are straightened. Should this not be done before the body stiffens, it is a cause of great embarrassment to the family, as it indicates their failure to care properly for their own. The body is washed by a close relative of the same sex, usually a father, brother, or son of a male; a mother, sister, or daughter of a female. The ritual of washing is done differently according to the stipulation of each sect. Then the body is wrapped in a cloth. It must be buried within 24 hours.

It is not considered proper to cry while the sufferer is still alive, but when he is clearly dead the female relatives of the deceased begin to wail. During the night before the burial, moreover, mullahs recite the Quran, if the family can afford to pay for this service. The very wealthy pay several mullahs or *qaaris* (men who have memorized the entire Quran) to recite the Quran through the night. In this case, they recite different portions all at the same time, so that the entire Quran can be recited in one night. (An edition of the Quran is published in fascicles for this kind of recitation.) At the end of the recitation of each section the mullah or qaari says "I have recited this on the behalf of ________," giving the deceased the merit in the hereafter. Those who recite through the night, besides their usual pay, are fed a meal by the host family.

Next day the body is carried on a cot to the cemetery by the male qawmi and friends of the deceased, each taking a turn at one of its corners along the way. The grave is dug by his qawmi. After the burial kinsmen and friends repeat parts of the Quran as prayers on his behalf. Three witnesses testify to his good character at the graveside. Imamis often eat a feast for the deceased at the grave. Finally, (mainly among the Sunnis) a few afghanis are given in small change to the poor who are present. The mullah imam is also paid his fee and in addition he sometimes keeps the small rug on which he said prayers at the graveside.

After a death the kinsmen are obliged to pay a courtesy visit on the family of the deceased. This is called a *faateya* (Arabic: *faatehah*). The family serves food to the visitors for the first three days after the death, and thereafter only tea. (Ismaili families serve no meals during the first three days, but afterwards slaughter a cow and distribute the parts raw to the kinsmen.) A visitor shows his grief by sitting far from the door and staying longer than others. To the family he is supposed to offer a few words of comfort: "He died, but we will all die too," "At least he was a good man: he was never a liar or thief, he never took another man's wife," "How lucky he was to have died on a Friday (or in a lucky month)," "Thank God he died with a good name, that he has many qawmi to bury him," "Thank God he didn't die in jail," etc. The visitor says a prayer for the dead after the meal or the tea that is served.

The faateya and several other meals that follow are known as *khayrat-e-morda,* "offering for the dead." A khayrat-e-morda feast is given on the seventh night, and also sometimes on the first Friday[4] after the death. This is no longer practiced among the Ismailis. At the next Id celebration it is also customary to give another khayrat-e-morda feast on behalf of the deceased, at which time visitors will say to their host, *Id-e-morda mubarak,* "a blessed Id for the dead."

One of the reasons for these feasts is that, as it is said, "the name of the deceased will not depart from the people's lips." It is important that many people should come to "do faateya" because this shows that the deceased and his family have many friends. Another reason for the feasts is to encourage the visitors to pray for the dead. This is an explicit purpose of the faateya meal and the other *khayrats* for the dead. "The value of the faateya," said one person, "is that the people pray for them." The mullah imam usually recites a prayer after the meal and all the men present raise their hands, palms up, and pray that God will forgive the deceased. One person said people come and pray no matter how they really feel about the dead person because they want to eat the food.[5]

Some people actually sponsor their own khayrat-e-morda before they die. The five children of an elderly wealthy woman gave a khayrat-e-morda for her before she died, because they believed a khayrat before death would be worth many times more than after death. After the khayrat she could not eat the khayrat food for anyone else. If she went to a khayrat feast she had to be fed by different food. After she dies, there may be another khayrat-e-morda for her.

Khayrat-e-morda feasts are sometimes undertaken at great cost to the surviving family. A certain man told me, for example, that the previous spring his wife had fallen through a faulty bridge and, as the river was at that time violently at flood tide, drowned. In order to get 2000 afghanis for the costs of the faateya for her, he had to turn over three *seyrs*[6] of his land as security for a loan (called *geraw*). Altogether he had only seven seyrs of land, barely enough for him to live on already, so this amounted to the loss of almost half of his already meager capital assets. Though technically he could regain the use of this land by repaying the loan, he was not likely to do so for some time, if ever, because his resources were below the threshold of survival. He was attempting to supplement his income by managing a tea shop, but had very few paying visitors.

The rituals associated with death, while obviously aimed at helping a social person depart from the group, also brings the surviving persons into social interaction and mutual obligation. The members of the group come to the house of the bereaved family to assist in the work and to offer condolences; food is

[4] This is the night before the day of Friday, as a night is counted as part of the day following it.

[5] Islamic tradition assures that prayers for the dead are efficacious. One scholar, for example, writes, "If a community of Muslims, a hundred strong, perform the *salaat* (funeral prayers) over a Muslim and all pray for his sins to be forgiven him, this prayer will surely be granted" (Muslim, Djanaliz, tradition 58; quoted in Gibb and Kramers 1953, article on *shafa'at*).

[6] A *seyr* is sixteen *paw* (= fifteen pounds). A seyr of land is a tract of land on which a seyr of seed is sown. The actual size varies according to the quality of the soil.

served; prayers are offered for the departed one as an expression of solidarity with the family who has served the food. In this way obligations are built up for future reciprocation as the circumstances require.

## SPECIAL RELIGIOUS OCCASIONS

Most of the social occasions already described have religious implications: the rite of circumcision, as mentioned before, initiates the young man into the body of adult believers who pray together; marriage is considered a religious duty, as it emulates the Prophet's example; and funeral ceremonies of course conform to religious prescriptions. Certain other ceremonies through which kinsmen are drawn together, however, are solely justified in religious terms. These are the Id festivities, the religious distributions known as *zakat* (alms), and other religious contributions known as *khayrats.*

### Id Celebrations

There are three festive occasions of the yearly calendar, Id-i-Fetr-i-Roza, "Festival of breaking the fast," Id-i-Qorban, "festival of sacrifice," and New Year's Day. Id-i-Fetr-i-Roza and Id-i-Qorban are essentially religious holidays, appearing on the lunar calendar and retrograding on the solar calendar 10 days per year. New Year's Day is based on the solar calendar and falls at the time of the vernal equinox (March 21). It is not actually a religious holiday to Sunnis, though many actually celebrate it in the same way as the other Id holidays, but to Imamis it is a day of special religious significance because on this day Ali took office as Calif. New Year's Day is therefore considered an Id (festival) and most of the routine observances of the day are the same as on the other Ids.

On an Id new clothes are worn, kinsmen of all sorts are visited, and prayers are said publicly. Also on an Id, food is shared. Usually on the night of an Id, each family eats its meal separately but sends gifts of cooked food from their own feast by the hand of a child to their relatives, affines as well as agnates. The next few days kinsmen may entertain each other in a reciprocal pattern known as *meymani dawra,* "feasting by turns (or circularly)." The families who participate in meymani dawra are those of the qawm community, usually terminological awdurs (FaBr) and awdurzadas (FaBrSo) of each other, but it may also include geographically close affines of the qawm community; sometimes closely interrelated qawm communities participate together in the meymani dawra. The following is a description of the meymani dawra:

> On one day we gather, maybe 15 or 20 people from six or seven households—we're all awdurs or awdurzadas of each other—to have a noon

meal, say, at my house. We eat rice, meat, tea, etc., and afterwards there will be music, singing and talking. Then at the end we pray that God will advance Islam everywhere, and reward all his people, and that He will make everyone at peace.

Then before we leave, one of the others calls out, "Tonight you must come to my house." So everyone comes that night and greets each other, and eats together. The host may spend 500 or a 1000 afghanis on this meal.

At that meal another calls out "Brothers, all of you, you have eaten here and elsewhere. Tomorrow you must eat at my place; you cannot go anywhere else. I have spent 500 afghanis for a sheep and as much more on other things, so I beg you to come to my house." Of course we want to eat there–and if he didn't invite us, it would annoy us–so we say, "Don't be unhappy, we'll come."

Then at that meal another gets up and says, "All of you are rich and I am poor among you. But if I should only have some barley-and-fava bean bread and a few bowls of buttermilk, would you come and eat?" Then we say, "of course, a thousand times, our brother, you are a good friend to everyone. We will come." But when we go, instead of bread made from fava bean and barley, buttermilk and the like, there is a great feast prepared for us: rice, meat, soup–everything in abundance. So we all think to ourselves, "I should do more than this poor man." And they all try to do twice as much, lest people think badly of them. . . .

The meymani dawra continues for three or four days until those households which can afford it have taken their turn.

## Religious Distributions

Distributions of food are made on the religious holidays and at certain other times during the year. The most important of these is the distribution of the fresh meat of a sheep, goat, or cow at Id-i-Qorban, "festival of sacrifice." This distribution is enjoined upon everyone who has enough to eat. Individual families slaughter a sheep or goat, but a few closely related families, usually brothers or awdurzadas (FaBrSo), sometimes jointly purchase and slaughter a cow. Before slaughter a prayer is recited over the animal, requesting God to accept it on their behalf.

The meat is shared with qawmi, neighbors and the poor. An effort is made to give to the poor, but in practice, whether to poor or rich, the distributions tend to flow to relatives. The distributions of fresh meat therefore are largely reciprocal exchanges among members of the kinship network.

Out of 30 families there may be 20 who slaughter a sacrifice but 10 families may be too poor. So these go to claim their meat from the others.

> The 20 families cut the meat into as many pieces as there are households and send it to each. The others also do the same, so no one is left out. But also they give something to a traveller on the road. They do this without asking anything about him, where he is from, his qawm, or anything. But the members of the different sects do their giving separately among themselves. They are one group and we are another group.

Another kind of distribution enjoined on all muslims who are financially eligible is the giving of alms, *zakat.* The zakat is called by the Sunnis *khayrat-i-fetr-i-roza,* "offering for the breaking of fast," because it is given on the first day of Id-i-fetr-i-roza. The zakat is a contribution to the poor. The ideal order of preference is, first, to a poor relative, then to a poor muslim neighbor, then, if there is neither of these, to any poor muslim, and failing all of these, to a poor unbeliever. The amount of the zakat is figured variously, but is approximately one-fortieth of one's yearly gain.

Khayrats are special distributions of goods, usually food, given without regard for a return in order to gain God's favor. A khayrat can be the gift of a candle or a flag to a shrine, a morsel of bread to an animal, or even (according to a story told by an Imami mullah) water to a thirsty plant in the name of God. Most often khayrats are offerings of food.

The khayrat aims to win God's favor in two ways. One is by the sacrifice which the giver sustains in giving the khayrat as a kind of penance. As it is given, the donor says, "May God accept this." The khayrat is also aimed at educing a prayer of thanksgiving and intercession from the beneficiary of the gifts, for it is believed the intercession of others results in the spiritual credit of the giver. At the end of a feast, for example, those who enjoy it will ask God's blessing on the host or, for example, on a sick child for whose deliverance the feast is offered. Thus, the importance of the intercession of kinsmen before God, mentioned elsewhere, is further indicated by the expenditures for khayrats.

The more expensive khayrats are given as cooked food. Khayrats may be cooked at a shrine and passed out to anyone present, or cooked at home and served to friends invited in, or secretly cooked and eaten by only a few, as a woman might do when afflicted by a malady she could only share with her closest friends.

Some khayrat feasts are given voluntarily—offered, for example, to obtain relief from a distress, or to achieve conception. Other khayrats are specifically enjoined upon the believer, such as the khayrat-e-morda, the zakat, and the qorbani distributions described above. The Imamis frequently give khayrat feasts on the night of the tenth of Moharram in memory of the slaughter of Hosayn and his friends. Sunnis and Ismailis serve sherbet or pudding to friends. At the time of the vernal and autumnal equinoxes, Imami families eat a pudding at a local shrine or at a mosque as a khayrat. Smaller amounts of food are sometimes given as khayrats at other times of the year in celebration of some religious event, such as the Prophet's birthday, or the twenty-seventh of the Arabic month of Rajab, when Ali is believed to have converted an acquisitive Jew by his generosity.

# BIBLIOGRAPHY


Adams, R. McC.

1962 Agriculture and Urban Life in Early Southwestern Iran. Science Vol. 136: 109-22.

1966 The Evolution of Urban Society. Aldine Publishing Co. Chicago.

Alland, A.

1967 Evolution and Human Behavior. Doubleday. Garden City, N.Y.

Aslanov, M. G., et al.

1969 Ethnography of Afghanistan. Translated by Mark and Gretta Slobin. *In:* Afghanistan: Some New Approaches, G. Grassmuch, L. W. Adamec, and F. H. Irwin, eds. University of Michigan Press. Ann Arbor.

Bacon, E.

1951*a* The Hazara Mongols of Afghanistan: A Study in Social Organization. Unpublished Ph.D. dissertation. University of California, Berkeley.

1951*b* The Inquiry into the History of the Hazara Mongols of Afghanistan. Southwestern Journal of Anthropology Vol. 7:230-47.

1958 Obok: A Study of Social Structure in Asia. Viking Fund Publications in Anthropology, No. 25. Wenner Gren Foundation for Anthropological Research.

Bailey, F.

1957 Caste and the Economic Frontier. Manchester University Press. Manchester.

1968 Parapolitical Structures. *In:* Local-Level Politics, M. J. Swartz, ed. Aldine Press. Chicago.

Banton, M. D.

1965 The Relevance of Models to Social Anthropology. ASA Monographs, No. 1. Praeger. New York.

Barnes, J. A.

1954 Class and Committees in a Norwegian Island Parish. Human Relations, Vol. 7:39-58.

Barrett, D. B.

1968 Schism and Renewal in Africa: An Analysis of Six Thousand Contemporary Religious Movements. Oxford University Press. London.

Barth, F.

1956 Ecologic Relationships Between Ethnic Groups in Swat, North Pakistan. American Anthropologist, Vol. 58:1079-89.

1959 Segmentary Opposition and the Theory of Games: A Study of Pathan Organization. Journal of the Royal Anthropological Institute, Vol. 89:5-21.

1961 Nomads of South Persia. Bulletin No. 8. Universitetets Etnografiske Museum. University of Oslo. (Published in the United States by Little, Brown. Boston.)

1966 Models of Social Organization. Royal Anthropological Institute, Occasional Papers, No. 23. Royal Anthropological Society of Great Britain and Ireland. London.

1969*a* Pathan Identity and Its Maintenance. *In:* Barth 1969*b*.

Barth, F., ed.

1969*b* Ethnic Groups and Boundaries: The Social Organization of Cultural Difference. Little, Brown. Boston.

Bassett, R. and C. Pellat

1960 Berbers: Religion. *In:* The Encyclopedia of Islam (new edition), B. Lewis, C. Pellat, and J. Schacht, eds. E. J. Brill. Leiden.

Bataillard, P.

1843 D' L'Apparition et de la Dispersion des Bhemiens en Europe. Bibliothetique de l'Ecole des Chartes, Vol. 1:14-15.

1875 The Affinities of Gypsies with the Jats. The Academy, Vol. 7:583-85.

Beardsley, R. R.

1964 Ecological and Social Parallels Between Rice-Growing Communities of Japan and Spain. *In:* Symposium on Community Studies in Anthropology, V. E. Garfield, ed. University of Washington Press. Seattle.

Bennett, J. W.

1969*a* Anthropological Research Bearing Upon the Use and Development of Water Resources. Written for the University of Kentucky Water Resources Institute Seminar on Water Resources and the Social Sciences (mimeo.). Washington University. St. Louis.

1969*b* Northern Plainsmen: Adaptive Strategy and Agrarian Life. Adline Publishing Co. Chicago.

Bourdieu, P.

1962 The Algerians. Translated by A. C. M. Ross. Beacon Press. Boston.

Bray, D.

1925 The Jat of Baluchistan. Indian Antiquity, Vol. 50:30-33.

Burnes, A.

1834 Travels into Bokhara, Being the Account of a Journey from India to Cabool, Tartary and Persia; Also, Narrative of a Voyage on the Indus . . . in the Years 1831, 1832, 1833. 3 Vols. John Murray. London.

1842 Cabool: A Personal Narrative of a Journey to, and Residence in, That City, in the Years 1836, 7, and 8. John Murray. London.

Burton, R.
1851 Sindh, and the Races that Inhabit the Valley of the Indus. W. H. Allen and Co. London.
1898 The Jew, the Gypsy and El Islam. Hutchinson and Co. London.

Campbell, J. K.
1964 Honor, Family and Patronage: A Study of Institutional, and Moral Values in a Greek Mountain Community. Oxford University Press. London.

Canfield, R. L.
in press The Ecology of Rural Ethnic Groups and the Spatial Dimensions of Power. American Anthropologist.

Caroe O.
1958 The Pathans: Five Hundred B.C. to A.D. Nineteen Hundred Fifty-Seven. Macmillan. London.

Cervin, V.
1952 Problems in the Integration of the Afghan Nation. Middle East Journal, Vol. 6:400-16.

Cohen, A.
1969 Custom and Politics in Urban Africa. University of California Press. Berkeley.

Cohen, Y.
1969 Social Boundary Systems. Current Anthropology, Vol. 10:103-26.

Coon, C. A.
1951 Caravan: The Story of the Middle East. Holt, Rinehart. New York.

Dollot, R.
1937 L'Afghanistan: Histoire, Description, Moers, et Coutumens. Payot. Paris.

Dupree, L.
1956 The Changing Character of South-Central Afghan Villages. Human Organization, Vol. 14, No. 4:26-29.

Easton, D.
1959 Political Anthropology. *In:* Bienniel Review of Anthropology, B. J. Siegel, ed. Stanford University Press. Stanford.
1965 A Systems Analysis of Political Life. John Wiley. New York.

Elphinstone, M.
1815 An Account of the Kingdom of Caubul, and Its Dependencies in Persia, Tartary and India, Comprising a View of the Afghaun Nation and a History of the Dooraunee Monarchy. John Murray. London.

Ferdinand, K.
1959 Preliminary Notes on Hazara Culture. Historiskfilosofiske Meddelelser Udgivet af Det Kongelige Danske Videnskabernes Selskab, Bind 37, Nr. 5. Ejnar Munksgaard. Kopenhagen.

Ferdinand, K. (cont.)
1962 Nomadic Expansion and Commerce in Central Afghanistan: A Sketch of Some Modern Trends. Folk, Vol. 4:123-59.

Ferrier, J. P.
1857 Caravan Journeys and Wanderings in Persia, Afghanistan, Turkestan and Beloochestan. John Murray. London.

Fletcher, A. C.
1965 Afghanistan: Highway of Conquest. Cornell University Press. Ithaca.

Furnival, J. S.
1948 Colonial Policy and Practice: A Comparative Study of Burma and Netherlands India. Cambridge University Press. Cambridge.

Geertz, C.
1957 Ritual and Social Change: A Javanese Example. American Anthropologist, Vol. 59:32-54.
1963 Peddlers and Princes: Social Development and Economic Change in Two Indonesian Towns. University of Chicago Press. Chicago.
1965 Social History of an Indonesian Town. MIT Press. Cambridge, Mass.

Gellner, E.
1970 Saints of the Atlas. University of Chicago Press. Chicago.

Gibb, H. A. R. and Kramers, J. H., eds.
1953 Shorter Encyclopedia of Islam. Cornell University Press. Ithaca.

Gibb, H. A. R., E. L. Provencal, and J. Schacht, eds.
1954- The Encyclopedia of Islam. E. J. Brill. Leiden.

Gluckman, M.
1963 Gossip and Scandal. Current Anthropology, Vol. 4:307-16.

Godard, A., Y. Godard, and J. Hackin
1928 Les Antiquites Bouddhiques de Bamiyan. Memoires de la Delegation Archeologique Francaise en Afghanistan. Vol. 2. Les Editions G. Van Oest. Paris.

Gonzales, N. L.
1970 The Neoteric Society. Comparative Studies in Society and History, Vol. 12, No. 1:1-13.

Government of India
1910 Gazetteer of Afghanistan. Part IV. Kabul. 4th edition. The Division of the Chief of Staff. Calcutta.

Gray, R. F.
1963 The Sonjo of Tanganijika: An Anthropological Study of an Irrigation-Based Society. Oxford University Press. London.

Grierson, G. A.
1889 Domes, Jats, and the Origins of Gypsies. Journal of Gypsy Lore, Vol. 1:71-76.

Haaland, G.
1969 Economic Determinants in Ethnic Processes. *In:* Barth 1969*b*.

Hackin, J., and C. J. Hackin
1933 Nouvelles Recherches Archeologiques a Bamian. Memoirs de la Delegation Archeologique Francaise en Afghanistan. Vol. 3. Les Editions G. Van Oest. Paris.

Hackin, J., C. J. Hackin, and J. Meunie
1959 Diverses Recherches Archeologiques in Afghanistan. Memoires de la Delegation Archeologique Francaise en Afghanistan. Vol. 8. Les Editions G. Van Oest. Paris.

Holloway, R. L.
1968 Human Aggression: The Need for a Species-Specific Framework. *In:* War: The Anthropology of Armed Conflict and Agression, M. H. Fried, M. Harris, and R. F. Murphy, eds. Natural History Press. Garden City, N.Y.

Harding. T. G.
1967 Voyagers of the Vitiaz Strait. University of Washington Press. Seattle.

Harlan, J.
1939 Central Asia: Personal Narrative of General Josiah Harlan, 1823-1841, F. E. Ross, ed. Luzac and Co. London.

Hudson, A. E. and E. Bacon
1941 Social Control and the Individual in Eastern Hazara Culture. *In:* Language, Culture and Personality: Essays in Honor of Edward Sapir, L. Spier, A. I. Hallowell, and S. S. Newman, eds. Sapir Memorial Publication Fund. Menasha, Wisconsin.

Irons, W. G.
1969 The Yomut Turkman: A Study of Kinship in a Pastoral Society. Unpublished Ph.D. Dissertation. University of Michigan. Ann Arbor.

Kakar, M. H.
1969 The Organization of the Central Government in Afghanistan under Amir Abdul Rahman, 1880-1906. Unpublished M. Phil. Thesis. School of Oriental and African Studies, University of London. London.

Lal, Mohana.
1834 Journal of a Tour Through the Panjab, Afghanistan, Turkistan, Khorasan, and Part of Persia in Company with Lieut. Burnes and Dr. Gerard. Baptist Mission Press. Calcutta.

Lambton, A. S. K.
1956 Quis Custodiet Custodes: Some Reflections on the Persian Theory of Government. Studia Islamica, Vol. 6:125-46.

Lattimore, O.
1956 The Frontier in Hisotry. *In:* Studies in Frontier History. Oxford University Press. New York.

Leach, Edmund
1954 Political Systems of Highland Burma: A Study of Kachin Social Structure. Harvard University Press. Cambridge, Mass.

Levi-Strauss, C.
1963 Structural Anthropology. Doubleday. Garden City, N.Y.

Lewis, B.
1953 Some Observations on the Significance of Heresy in the History of Islam. Studia Islamica, Vol. 53, No. 1:43-63.

Masson, C.
1842 Narrative of Various Journeys in Beloochistan, Afghanistan, and the Panjab, Including a Residence in Those Countries from 1826 to 1836. 3 vols. Richard Bentley. London.

Mayer, A. C.
1966 The Significance of Quasi-Groups in the Study of Complex Societies. *In:* The Social Anthropology of Complex Societies, M. Banton, ed. Praeger. New York.

Mir Munshi, S. M. K., ed.
1900 The Life of Abdur Rahman, Amir of Afghanistan. 2 vols. John Murray. London.

Morse, R. M.
1965 Recent Research on Latin American Urbanization: A Select Survey with Commentary. Latin American Research Review, Vol. 1:35-74.

Musil, Alois
1928 The Manners and Customs of the Rwala Bedouins. American Geographical Society Oriental Explorations and Studies, No. 6. American Geographical Society. New York.

Peristiany, J. G., ed.
1966 Honour and Shame: The Values of Mediterranean Society. University of Chicago Press. Chicago.

Planhol, X. de
1959 The World of Islam. Cornell University Press. Ithaca.

Porter, P. W.
1965 Environmental Potentials and Economic Opportunities: A Background for Cultural Adaptation. American Anthropologist, Vol. 67, No. 2:409-20.

Price, D.
1821 Chronological Retrospect: Or Memoirs of the Principal Events of Mohammedan History. 3 Vols. J. Booth, London.

Raverty, H. G.
1888 Notes on Afghanistan and Part of Baluchistan, Geographical, Ethnological, and Historical. G. E. Eyre and W. Spottiswoode. London.

Sahlins, M. D.
1961 The Segmentary Lineage: An Organization of Predatory Expansion. American Anthropologist, Vol. 63:322-43.
1964 Culture and Environment. *In:* Horizons in Anthropology, S. Tax, ed. Aldine Publishing Co. Chicago.
1965*a* On the Ideology and Composition of Descent Groups. Man, Vol. 65:104-07.
1965*b* On the Sociology of Primitive Exchange. *In:* Banton 1965.
1968 Tribesman. Prentice-Hall, Inc. Englewood Cliffs, N.J.

Sangree, W. H.
1966 Age, Prayer and Politics in Tiriki, Kenya. Oxford University Press. London.

Schurmann, H. F.
1962 The Mongols of Afghanistan: An Ethnography of the Mongols and Related Peoples of Afghanistan. Mouton. 'S-Gravenhage.

Steward, J., ed.
1955 Irrigation Civilizations: A Comparative Study: A Symposium on Method and Result in Cross-Cultural Regularities. Pan American Union. Washington, D.C.

Sykes, P. M.
1910 Persian Jats. Journal of Gypsy Lore, Vol. 3:320.

Vambrey, A.
1864 Travels in Central Asia, Being an Account of a Journey from Teheran Across the Turkoman Desert on the Eastern Shore of the Caspian to Khiva, Bokhara and Samarcand, Performed in the Year 1863. John Murray. London.

Vavilov, N. I. and D. D. Bukinich
1929 Zemledel'cheikiy Afghanistan 33 to the Bulletin of Applied Botany, Genetics and Plant Breeding. Leningrad.

Ward, B. E.
1965 Varieties of the Conscious Model: The Fishermen of South China. *In:* Banton 1965.
1966 Sociological Self-Awareness: Some Uses of Conscious Models. Man, Vol. 1:201-15.

Wilbur, D. N., ed.
1956 Afghanistan: Its People, Its History, Its Culture. Human Relations Area Files. New Haven.

Wittfogel, K.
1957 Oriental Despotism: A Comparative Study of Total Power. Yale University Press. New Haven.

Wolf, E. R.
1956 Aspects of Group Relations in a Complex Society: Mexico. American Anthropologist, Vol. 58:1965-78.
1966 Peasants. Prentice-Hall, Inc. Englewood Cliffs, N.J.

Wolf, E. and A. Palerm
1955 Irrigation in the Old Acolhua Domain. Southwestern Journal of Anthropology, Vol. 11:265-81.

Wolfe, N. H.
1963 The Valley of Bamian. Afghan Tourist Organization. Kabul.

Wood, J.
1841 A Personal Narrative of a Journey to the Source of the River Oxus by the Route of the Indus, Kabul and Badakhshan. Performed Under the Sanction of the Supreme Government of India in the Years 1836, 1937, and 1838. John Murray. London.